*Don't Look Away*

# Don't Look Away

Saying Yes to the One

DON BREWSTER

*Foreword by* Mira Sorvino

CASCADE *Books* • Eugene, Oregon

DON'T LOOK AWAY
Saying Yes to the One

Copyright © 2024 Don Brewster. All rights reserved. Except for brief quotations in critical publications or reviews, no part of this book may be reproduced in any manner without prior written permission from the publisher. Write: Permissions, Wipf and Stock Publishers, 199 W. 8th Ave., Suite 3, Eugene, OR 97401.

Cascade Books
An Imprint of Wipf and Stock Publishers
199 W. 8th Ave., Suite 3
Eugene, OR 97401

www.wipfandstock.com

PAPERBACK ISBN: 978-1-6667-7926-4
HARDCOVER ISBN: 978-1-6667-7927-1
EBOOK ISBN: 978-1-6667-7928-8

*Cataloguing-in-Publication data:*

Names: Brewster, Don, author. | Sorvino, Mira, foreword.
Title: Don't look away : saying yes to the one / Don Brewster.
Description: Eugene, OR: Cascade Books, 2024 | Includes bibliographical references.
Identifiers: ISBN 978-1-6667-7926-4 (paperback) | ISBN 978-1-6667-7927-1 (hardcover) | ISBN 978-1-6667-7928-8 (ebook)
Subjects: LCSH: Human trafficking—Prevention. | Human trafficking—Religious aspects—Christianity. | Brewster, Don, 1954–.
Classification: HQ281 .B742 2024 (print) | HQ281 .B742 (ebook)

Scripture quotations marked NIV are taken from The Holy Bible, New International Version®, NIV®. Copyright © 1973, 1978, 1984, 2011 by Biblica, Inc.® Used by permission. All rights reserved worldwide.

Scripture quotations marked NLT are taken from the *Holy Bible,* New Living Translation, copyright © 1996, 2004, 2015 by Tyndale House Foundation. Used by permission of Tyndale House Publishers, Carol Stream, Illinois 60188. All rights reserved.

To Bridget Brewster my bride and ministry co-founder.
Your great love and compassion inspire so many,
especially me.

And to the staff, volunteers, and supporters of AIM—
without you there would be no stories to write.

When the Lord saw her,
his heart overflowed with compassion.
—Luke 7:13 NLT

# CONTENTS

Foreword by Mira Sorvino  ix

Introduction: Slaves Turned Abolitionists  xvii

Chapter 1: Cambodia  1

Chapter 2: The Decision  8

Chapter 3: Who's on Our Team?  13

Chapter 4: Princesses  18

Chapter 5: Lessons in Love  24

Chapter 6: Davids  33

Chapter 7: Open to the Unexpected, both Good and Bad  42

Chapter 8: SWAT  53

Chapter 9: Svay Pak  61

Chapter 10: Jesus Moves to Svay Pak  67

Chapter 11: Going Back  83

Chapter 12: Fighting Back  91

## Contents

Chapter 13: Conflict  98

Chapter 14: Why?  105

Acknowledgments  113

Appendix 1: Sophia's Story  115

Appendix 2: Linda's Story  119

Appendix 3: Overcoming the Porn Pandemic in the Church  122

Appendix 3a: Addiction  144

Appendix 3b: Caleb Miller, CEO and Co-Founder of Regenerate  148

Appendix 3c: Recommended Resources  156

# FOREWORD

## by Mira Sorvino

When Don and Bridget Brewster asked me to write a foreword for their book, I felt humbled, and somewhat intimidated. Who was I to write about people who were literally the holiest people I knew, that in every fiber of their being, walk the walk in terms of living out the calling of Jesus Christ? I have literally described Don as being the closest thing to a saint I have ever encountered. But sharing my experience of their light could help others aspire to live the same way, so here is my attempt.

I have been involved in the fight against human trafficking since 2004, when I learned about it as part of my role as a Stop Violence Against Women campaign spokesperson for Amnesty International. I was horrified to learn the abolition of the legal chattel slavery of the past was not the end—slavery had just gone underground, becoming the second most profitable criminal enterprise in the world, one worth 150 billion dollars a year. It is estimated over 40 million people live in slavery today, more than at any other point in recorded human history. Seventy-one percent of its victims are women and girls and one of every four victims is a child.[1] Yet horrifyingly only .04 percent of human trafficking survivors are currently discovered and identified—a less than 1 percent chance of breaking out of a life of agony, whether in labor or sex trafficking.

Combatting this scourge quickly rose the forefront of my activist efforts, especially after I began meeting with people who had endured this torture: I saw in their eyes an excoriation, as though they had seen something no one else could comprehend in terms of the depravity, the abject

---

1. Stats found at: https://www.ilo.org/global/topics/forced-labour/lang--en/index.htm.

cruelty and torturous monstrosity at the hands of other human beings. The only comparison I could possibly make was to Holocaust survivors.

In 2009 I was asked by the United Nations Office on Drugs and Crime (UNODC) to become a goodwill ambassador in the worldwide fight against human trafficking. I was inducted then and have remained in my post through the present day—it continues to be one of the great honors and privileges of my life. It quickly became my goal to interview as many survivors and aid workers as possible, to gather their stories as tools to better advocate for their needs when they could not be present themselves. Of course any meaningful actions to combat human trafficking should have at their front and center survivor leaders; I simply seek to bolster them with the collected testimonies of people from many countries and situations whose wisdom and stories can sway policymakers.

One salient feature struck me in all of the stories. The traffickers did not generally enslave and mistreat people out of an *a priori* prejudice against a minority—the inhumanity was not doled out from some sense of racial or religious superiority. Traffickers saw opportunity, plain and simple, in each of their victims, to make an enormous amount of money. And then they treated them without any empathy at all. As though they were not human. As though they were things. As one human trafficker told to me in Spain, "A woman or girl is like this glass, she is a mercantile object to be traded or sold. In the old days of pimping we used to have to create a whole fiction, that we loved them, that we were building a common future together; now we just threaten them with harm to themselves and their families and make them work by force."

The savagery, especially to children, is mind-boggling, dangerously mind-numbing—to think that babies can be raped, that someone can take pleasure in sexually abusing tiny or prepubescent children, that they can punish teenagers in a brothel for insubordination with beatings, maiming, or death is so hard for our minds and hearts to take that it can repel well-meaning do-gooders, make them look away. But this we cannot do. And this is precisely where Don and Bridget Brewster come in.

In 2012, the CNN Freedom Project, with whom I had collaborated several times prior, reached out to ask if I would be willing to be the on-the-ground host of a documentary about child sex trafficking in Cambodia, in one of the poorest of the poor neighborhoods that had become an epicenter for pedophile purchases of children: Svay Pak. They said the government had promised that the neighborhood had been cleared of such practices,

## Foreword

but the reality was that it was ongoing. I immediately signed on, but with a heaviness in my heart, because I was afraid of what I would confront there. The year before, I had shot a feature film in nearby Thailand, on a related topic, called *Trade of Innocents*. The film was supposed to be based in Cambodia, but the government wouldn't let us film there, perhaps due to sensitivity about their image. I used the time to deepen my knowledge about trafficking in the region, working with the very excellent UNODC field office there, being briefed by the FBI, and touring the area with very capable guides from local NGOs that fought child and adult sex trafficking. It was very sobering, and I knew Cambodia would be a similar if not more harrowing experience.

When we got to Cambodia, the dichotomy between the wealthiest classes and the poor was extremely striking. When we walked through the shanty town areas of Svay Pak, where families of ten would live in tiny one-room shacks set atop mounds of garbage, with no indoor plumbing and temporary roofs, with dogs wandering through mud streets scratching at thousands of fleas, or as we boated through the floating villages where paperless Vietnamese immigrants lived trying to eke out a meager living raising fish under their dilapidated homes, I was exposed to a level of poverty I had not seen before. Young men zoomed by on motos with tiny girls dressed in Catholic school uniforms, and my stomach filled with dread as to their destination—were they being brought somewhere to be raped by a pedophile? The squalor outside was only bested by the probable goings-on inside the buildings.

And then the ray of light: I was led to meet Don and Bridget Brewster. They came out and met me smack in the middle of Svay Pak, in front of an enormous, colorful building called Rahab's House, and I was struck with their casual attire and kind smiles. They showed me around their facilities, filled with children in classes, in church, and many local people running rooms, as well as American college and grad students volunteering on campus. The building had formerly been owned by local traffickers, and now was repurposed to be a place of joyful healing and learning.

Then Don took me on a walk through the streets. As we approached a group of men sitting around outside a small building playing cards, Don said these men were local traffickers, and that they would not only traffic other people's children but their *own children*. They lounged around in the heat, looking completely unconcerned that a film crew was pointed at them. I, being a ridiculous person, started getting so incensed that I began yelling at them in English, which they didn't understand, that it was "not okay" to sell kids for sex, that the world was watching. It was an exercise in futility only serving to vent my grief, which Don very sympathetically listened to. I revealed that I was afraid of what I would find here, and to know that this inhumane torture of children went on "every day!" In that moment, I unwittingly provided the documentary with its name, *Every Day in Cambodia*.

Don went on to explain that when he and Bridget had first moved into the neighborhood, *100 percent* of the children here were eventually trafficked, especially as pedophiles, both foreign and local, paid very high prices for children's virginities. It had become a lamentable endemic practice for families impoverished by extreme loan sharks to sell their children to pay down their impossible debts.

But the Brewsters' organization, Agape International Missions (AIM), was making a dent in these sordid statistics in human misery. And, as we walked back towards Rahab's House, Don pointed out a remarkable establishment they had created: The Lord's Gym. They had found a local kickboxing champion and third-generation Christian, an anomaly in the country Pol Pot had decimated, to run the gym designed to entice young toughs in the neighborhood. In order to work out there the young men had to abide by his rules and ethics. Being a registered gym, its fighters were allowed to fight in nationally televised fights. What ended up happening is that sixteen young men, formerly among the most ruthless child traffickers, had foresworn their old life and thousands of dollars a month in exchange for the honor of being national athletes. Due to the mentorship of their coach, these young men became anti-trafficking advocates, truly having revolutionized their lives from doing extreme wrong to fighting for good.

I was floored. The hatred (yes, I ashamedly admit it) I felt for the men I had just yelled at would not have allowed me to see beyond their crimes to the possibility of their redemption. Don Brewster could and did. He truly was able to turn the other cheek and love his enemy, and in so doing, was using God's love as an instrument for extraordinary love and change. The ingenuity and generosity coupled in the creation of the gym really astounded me—I had never really seen Christ's intent come to life in such a way.

Later I was able to accompany Don and Bridget as they led a highly expectant group of rescued teenage girls to their new home: a former brothel that had been converted into a beautiful, colorfully decorated dorm for them. To top it all off, there was a gorgeous rooftop terrace for them to safely hang out in together. To see the delight in their faces as they bounced on the beds or hear their pure, beautiful voices as they joined hands together on the roof and sang songs of praise brought tears to my eyes.

Don and Bridget love on these girls until they feel like they are people of worth, something that has been brutally taken from them. When I called Don asking for help on recommendations on a speech I was preparing to present at the Vatican on behalf of UNODC for the second annual conference of clergy and law enforcement collaborating to fight trafficking, he reiterated that the most important element of treatment was love. "The greatest among these is love . . ." Bridget and Don heap God's love on them and it in turn works miracles of growth and happiness and possibility in them.

At the same time, Don does not give up or shirk from the hard and scary tasks. He blazed a trail getting the Cambodian government to work hand in hand with AIM where other NGOs had failed. In what seemed to be an impossible task, he not only raised an extraordinary amount of money and expert manpower but got the government to agree to allow AIM to create and train an elite SWAT team comprised of local Cambodian law enforcement to eliminate the corruption that had thwarted their previous raids on brothels. (A policeman in the region had told me that money was so scarce in his department and salaries so low that if he wanted to investigate a trafficking subject, he and other officers would have to pool close to a month's salary to pay for the gas for the moto just to travel to do the work.) This team has been extraordinarily successful and has saved thousands of people to date.

I saw the love Bridget has for the girls they attend to as I conducted heart-wrenching interviews where I gently tried to elicit from them the circumstances of their mothers selling them. Bridget has become the mother figure for all souls helped by AIM. I knew the personal sacrifice she and Don had to pay in order to leave their lives and their extended family of children and grandchildren in the States.

Yet their commitment is constant and true, fearless in its scope. Don took me and the CNN cameraman on a tour of some of the red light districts and "KTVs"(karaoke bars fronting for brothels that sold underage girls). We drove into the basement of a very large one and our interpreter noted in surprise the government plates on many of the super expensive Range Rovers and Maybachs. We took the elevator up to the fifth floor where Don suspected they kept the youngest girls. We all posed as buyers, a sort of strange triangle of two men and myself out for a night of depravity. We were walked in front of a large glass window, a sort of "fishbowl," beyond which on white stadium seats between twenty-five and forty young girls sat. Heavily made up and sexily dressed, it was impossible to tell if they were fourteen or twenty. But they all wore numbers, something I had seen in a Thai sex show club in the red light district in Bangkok, something that was also described to me by an American friend who was trafficked at eleven in a warehouse in North Carolina. All the kids had numbers on their clothes, so that the buyer could just pick one and pay to take them to a cubicle and rape them.

As we stood there I raised my hand with my phone in it—I was tempted to take a picture but couldn't dare. At that moment the mamasan, or madam, or female trafficking enforcer (women are far more commonly involved as perpetrators of human trafficking than in almost any other crime—see Ghislaine Maxwell—usually having graduated out of having been exploited themselves, reportedly among the most ruthless) started screaming "She take a picture!" and several bodyguards swarmed us. As we beat a fast path back to the elevator, Don turned to the cameraman urgently. "Did you see that?!" We both said no. "One of the doors just opened down the hall and a whole group of little children poured out to see what was going on!"

Later that night we went to another mid-sized KTV and rented a large room with an oversized TV and three "hostesses" in long satin gowns, from whom we were meant to buy food and drink, and supposedly, them, although we were equipped with microphones and sang along to the onscreen karaoke. Don started speaking to one whom he realized was a Vietnamese immigrant, and while I made big sport of singing vigorously, he shared his iPhone with her and gave her his headphones. On it he played for her a video of one of his staff members, a young woman who had formerly been exploited, speaking in Vietnamese, about how there was a better life waiting for her, with kind people and an education and an opportunity for decent work, that she didn't have to spend her life abused, at risk of contracting AIDS, in debt bondage to her traffickers, who could kill her. Don spent hours earning her trust. She had come from the countryside and was there to earn money to send back to her family. I know after I left Cambodia he said they had struck up a communication, with her cautiously interested in investigating the possibility of leaving the life and coming to AIM. Watching him for hours that night working to help one girl, despite the risk

## FOREWORD

of discovery, and possible violence from the traffickers who would not be happy at him taking away a source of their livelihood, was so inspirational. He and Bridget never ever give up.

This spirit of perseverance, courage, and a hunger for justice also manifests itself in the girls AIM works with. You will read of the magnificent courage of Toha, who with their help managed to testify in court against the brothel managers who enslaved her, and in a historic first, was able to get them convicted to serious jail time. This pint-sized, gentle-voiced girl rose above the extremely difficult odds of her own mother selling her into slavery to become a heroic changemaker.

In the years since I made the documentary with CNN, Don and Bridget have not rested on their laurels, instead expanding to create an extraordinary school in the heart of Svay Pak that can accommodate over a thousand students, offering kindergarten through postsecondary education: an incredible game changer that can in one generation lift whole families out of poverty. Unannounced weekly home checks of every family that has a student in the school ensure that neither they nor their siblings are being trafficked. Meanwhile, both loans and employment are given to the parents, so they can reverse the trend of exploiting their children and provide for them instead. All of this while spreading the incredible love of Jesus Christ!

Don and Bridget are transforming the community from the inside out with a holistic approach that addresses every angle, moving from the original work of triage and rehabilitation to prevention and community and morals building. They are changing the culture and raising the value of humanity, empathy, and the honor of doing honest, safe work. Redeeming the honor of the exploited children in the eyes of the community by providing them with educations and job skills, but even more importantly restoring their honor in their own eyes as they learn to see themselves as God sees them. As beautiful beings full of potential and lovability.

You too will be transformed by the love of God working through Don and Bridget. We all can answer that higher call—it is a blessing that keeps on multiplying and transforming not only our own lives but the lives of others around us. I am so grateful to know them, to be witness to the miracles that God has wrought through their ardent partnership. I can't wait to see what it will inspire in you.

Mira Sorvino
Los Angeles, California, June 7, 2023

# INTRODUCTION: SLAVES TURNED ABOLITIONISTS

**NOTE**

THROUGHOUT THIS BOOK THE names of the girls whose stories are shared have been changed for their protection. For the same reason the details of the abuse they suffered are not shared. What remains is the ugly truth and the transformed beauty of healing fueled by unconditional love. Some girls were knowingly sold to Western pedophiles or brothels by their mothers, fathers, grandparents, aunts, or uncles. The heavy shackles of poverty forced others to sell themselves, as they could no longer bear to hear the cries of hunger coming from their siblings or endure their mothers quaking in fear over the money owed to violent loan sharks. Each one of them was abused daily in unimaginable ways, some for a few days, others for a few years. There is a part of me that wants you to know the details, fearing without them it's too easy to miss the miracles each girl represents. My prayer is you will not only see the miracles, but also see how you can be a part of such miracles. All proceeds from the sale of this book will be used to care for the rescued victims of child sex trafficking in Cambodia.

**AMY**

Like most Cambodian girls, Amy was told that she existed for the benefit of her family. Like most Cambodian girls, she grew up with no dreams of her own. Life was a constant battle for simple survival. She didn't have a voice of her own, she didn't have any options: she had to do whatever her parents demanded. Which is why, when Amy was eight years old, she couldn't even fight it when her parents sold her to Michael Pepe, an American pedophile

## Introduction: Slaves Turned Abolitionists

living in Cambodia. She was told that it was a job, that she would be earning wages, that this was simply how the world works. The family had debts to repay, and it was her responsibility to do whatever it took to help her family.

Amy was never told that children shouldn't be sold for the pleasure of some and the profit of others.

She continued to struggle for survival until June 21, 2006, when Amy and six other enslaved girls were rescued in a raid. The US federal agents who rescued her said it was the worst case of child abuse they had ever seen. Michael Pepe was extradited to the US to await trial, while Amy and four other girls came to live at our Agape International Missions (AIM) home for the rescued victims of child sex trafficking.

For the first time in her life, Amy felt safe. She felt it was the beginning of something great. She was told that she was special, a princess, the daughter of the King of the universe. She learned through therapy she was valuable and worthy of love. We can tell these rescued girls about their worth day after day for years; however, it might never be felt beyond a cognitive level. With all of the trauma they've experienced, words are simply not enough. It was through experiencing the persevering love of our Cambodian staff, through being *actually treated as* valuable and lovable, that Amy and the other girls slowly came to believe that they had value and purpose. I probably would not believe that such healing was possible if my wife, Bridget, and I hadn't seen it so many times.

At age nine, Amy and four other girls traveled to the US to testify against their abuser. They knew that their voices mattered and that they could do something to fight the injustices they had experienced. Based on their courageous testimony, Michael Pepe was convicted and sentenced to 220 years in prison.

Today, Amy is a modern-day abolitionist caring for rescued victims of sex trafficking in Cambodia. She's one of many young women who have been transformed from a horribly abused victim to a modern-day abolitionist—more than surviving, they are thriving.

"I was taught to help other people even when I had nothing," Amy says today. "I am motivated by the hope that me being there and my experience can influence the girls and change their belief and find their identity. I want them to feel empowered and to see who they are and who they can potentially be. I wrestle with the fear of 'what if?' What if it's too hard being in the same place that traumatized me? What if I'm just not able to help? But we can always give something."

Introduction: Slaves Turned Abolitionists

## BETTY

Betty was born in Phnom Penh and grew up in the infamous "Anarchy Building." This massive white building was built in the 1960s as a utopian housing community for artists. It was totally incongruous with the rest of the city, which mainly consisted of small shacks. It was meant to be an impressive building, but long before Betty was born, it had become a towering, self-contained ghetto. In the midst of an impoverished region, the Anarchy Building stood five stories tall—a dilapidated tenement that housed crime, prostitution, and devastation. Even the police were afraid to go in it.

No one should spend their childhood in a place like this.

Betty lived with her mom in extreme poverty until she turned twelve years old. Her mom sent her off with a lady she didn't know for a job cleaning a house and washing the family's clothes. After only a couple of months, Betty discovered that she had, in fact, been sold into sex slavery. As it turns out, her mother knew exactly what was happening, and was actually (minimally) profiting from the arrangement.

As a young virgin, Betty was valuable, extremely valuable. The home in which she was forced to live was part of a sex trafficking ring. The woman who owned the home had connections with American and European pedophiles who were looking for young girls. Betty and other girls lived as prisoners in the house until a pedophile wanted one or more of the girls, then they would be sent to a guest house to do whatever these men demanded.

It was a traumatic and harrowing existence. Betty, like so many other girls, was forced to have sex with these men, typically five times every day, for $20. Literally $20 per rape! Every time she tried to protest, begging the woman not to force her to go, she would be screamed at and beaten. While she lived in that house, she was in constant physical and psychological pain. The woman who imprisoned her by day and pimped her out by night had three children who also functioned as jailers. They kept constant watch on Betty and the other girls, who were never allowed to leave the house except to be raped by pedophiles. She cried and begged for the horrific abuse to stop, but the woman told her that if she tried to escape, they would hurt her family.

The depth of such evil is beyond what our imaginations can conceive.

One day Betty and two of her friends were sent to have sex with two Westerners. She describes feeling happy as she left the house, though she didn't know why. Something felt different to her. At the hotel, the two

Western men began asking the three girls about their lives. As they answered, the men asked a question they had never heard before:

"Do you want to leave the place where you live?"

What the girls couldn't have known is an anti-trafficking NGO (non-government organization) had been working with the Cambodian National Police to shut down the specific operation that was trafficking Betty. So much intelligence gathering goes into a rescue operation of this nature, and the execution of the plan is always touch and go, at best. There's a risk that the traffickers will get suspicious—or be tipped off and go underground, which is often the case. For Betty, everything came together to execute a successful rescue.

When Betty came to live with us in our aftercare home, she was in great pain. She didn't trust anyone. Why would she? In addition to her family betraying her and her captors abusing her, she had gone through two other aftercare homes that were unable to adequately deal with the manipulation skills Betty had developed in order to survive. But our house moms, social workers, and counselors loved her unconditionally. Their love persisted no matter how awful she was to them (and she was plenty awful at first). Our team truly believed Betty was a child of God, a child of great value. While they would never have tolerated that type of hurtful behavior from their own children, they knew how much Betty needed their persevering love.

Betty, like all the girls in our restoration homes, was invited to listen when we would share about Jesus. We have never forced any of the girls in our homes to listen or respond, but we believe that unconditional love cannot be fully understood without understanding Jesus, and we believe this is essential to the healing process. Over the years, we saw Betty soften and change. She was beginning to understand and accept that God loves her, that she is in fact special—a daughter of the true King. She began to accept the love we gave her and to trust that we truly wanted what was best for her. She gave her heart to Jesus and became an incredible blessing in the restoration home. That day she said, "Many times you told me I was special, but I did not believe you. Today I know I am special!"

After beginning her studies that would lead her down the path of earning a college degree in the US, Betty came to us and said, "I want to be able to help other girls." It is a beautiful picture when someone who has been plucked from hell decides to return to the fight and save others. It's more than that; knowing each girl's story in detail, I know it's a miracle!

Introduction: Slaves Turned Abolitionists

Betty began going directly into the brothels and clubs to talk to girls who were still being prostituted! She wanted to show them that they could have a new life. Who could make a better case for this than someone who was living proof of the possibility of a new life? It's hard to imagine the amount of courage it takes for someone who was once imprisoned in brothels to go straight back and try to help others.

It is said the older girls (from their late teens into their twenties and thirties) stay in the brothels and clubs by their own choice. It's true they are no longer physically captive like the younger girls. It's worse! It's one thing to go into a brothel, kick down a door, scoop up a little girl, and run out of the building. It's actually much more difficult to go to a girl who's in the middle of all this horror and convince her that there's a way out. Her chains are not made of steel, they are stronger: built out of fear, shame, and poverty. Hers are chains of utter hopelessness. Betty goes into the brothels to break those stronger chains through telling the story of her new life and being a conduit of Jesus' love for her. She is amazingly successful.

## CAROL

Throughout Asia, there is a belief that if you're having bad luck, sex with a virgin can turn your luck around. This superstition ensures that sex traffickers will always find a market near the casinos.

Carol was twelve years old when her mother sold her virginity. She was taken to a hotel near a casino in Phnom Penh, where a man from China purchased her virginity in an attempt to change his gambling luck (among other reasons). The man purchased Carol for three days. She was trapped in the hotel while the man came back from the casino to rape her as many times as he wanted. Tragically, this is not uncommon in Cambodia.

After those three days of hell, Carol was sent back to her mother. But this didn't end her suffering—her nightmare continued. In the communities where sex trafficking is prevalent, the shame of what happens to a trafficked girl falls less upon the mother who sold her and the man who abused her, but more on the girl who has now lost her virginity.

After a couple of weeks of bearing this shame in her home community, the same man from China wanted to buy Carol again. Just a few weeks prior, when she was a virgin, she would have been sold for $8,000–$10,000. With most of the money going to the trafficker, Carol's mom would have received $1,000 or less. Now that she was no longer a virgin, she was being

## Introduction: Slaves Turned Abolitionists

sold for only a couple of hundred dollars. When her mom sold her the second time, she was pocketing around $50. Carol spent a couple more days being raped by this man then returned home. By this time the cruel and shameful experience that Carol endured stole her innocence and stripped her of all value in the eyes of everyone in her community and family. So her mom sold her to a brothel a couple of hours away.

Carol had learned of AIM through some other girls, and she found a way to call us. One day we received a phone call saying, "I'm trapped in a brothel! Please come rescue me!"

I didn't know exactly what the situation was, but I told her, "We'll be there in two days."

Why wait two days? In the past when we received a call like this we immediately responded with the only form of rescue then available to us. We would go to the brothel and say we wanted to buy the girl. Someone would bring the girl out, then we would jump in our car with her and take off. Of course we didn't pay. The results were great for the one girl who was rescued, but the brothel would stay opened, unfazed. Another girl would simply take her place.

So now we waited two days so we could provide the intel Carol gave us to another organization who specialized in working with the Cambodian police. They specialized in conducting rescues that resulted in the shutting down of brothels and the arrest of traffickers. A plan was developed to rescue Carol. Despite my unwarranted confidence the owner of the brothel was tipped off to the rescue plan. The owner reacted and made a plan of his own: Relocate the girls to an unknown location.

After moving the girls into hiding, the brothel owner entered Carol's room and told her, in no uncertain terms, "I own you. I own the police. You're never leaving this place!"

Carol looked him in the eyes and said, "I'm not worried about it. AIM is coming to get me." So brave. So naive.

This man, who had just told Carol he owned her and the police, who made his living off of keeping girls like Carol enslaved, responded, "Well, if they're coming, then you can go." Inexplicably, he put her on a bus and sent her to us.

This would not be the last time we would see God accomplish the impossible without any regard for the wisdom or foolishness of our plans. It seemed clear to us that day these evil traffickers were more afraid of Jesus than of the police, because he certainly wasn't afraid of us.

## Introduction: Slaves Turned Abolitionists

Carol spent a total of twenty-two days in the brothel before being "rescued." This is a relatively short amount of time—in fact I thought she was so blessed to have spent just twenty-two days as a sex slave. Other girls are often enslaved for years. Evidence later recovered revealed that in those twenty-two days, Carol was raped 198 times! This instilled in us a sense of urgency that would eventually lead to a whole new method of rescue and protocol.

For the time being Bridget and I had "22 Days" tattooed on our forearms so we'd never forget the trauma a girl experiences in just one day of slavery.

Carol began to heal in one of our restoration homes, eventually working in one of AIM's employment centers where we provide safe and sustainable employment for girls being reintegrated into Cambodian society. Though she had so much shame when she was first rescued, she experienced Jesus' love and through him found that all of her shame had been removed.

She mattered to Jesus, which means that she matters. Period. This realization of her self-worth led Carol to take more steps of faith. She decided that she wanted to be a social worker so she could help to rescue and restore girls who were experiencing the pain she knew so well. She studied evenings and today is part of a first responders social worker team who are essential in rescue efforts. Carol's transformation led me to add to my "22 Day" tat. Underneath it says "Love Never Fails," another good reminder in the long fight against child sex trafficking.

## DONNA

Donna was nine years old when she, like Amy, was sold by her mother to the American pedophile Michael Pepe. In a few short months, she was raped ninety to a hundred times. Donna was unique in that she kept fighting and crying longer than the other girls, so much so that she became a bother to Pepe. He eventually sold her to another American pedophile named Terry Smith, who had warrants out for his arrest in the United States for abusing children there. Smith had purchased her not only for his pleasure, but for the pleasure of the customers at his bar, Tramp's Place, in Sihanoukville. He forced her, and other girls, to dance seductively on tabletops at the bar and recorded the activity. He later posted the videos online. One of the girls managed to escape and through God's grace was found by a Cambodian police officer. This officer launched a raid and rescued Donna and the other girls. Donna entered our restoration home and like the others experienced the healing and transformative love of Jesus.

Like the other girls rescued from Michael Pepe, Donna came to the United States to testify against him. And like the other girls she was able to return to the States. Donna graduated from high school, then graduated from cosmetology school, receiving her license to work in the United States. She was extremely successful and earned enough to travel back to Cambodia and help other girls who have experienced the hell of sex trafficking. On her first trip back to Cambodia, Donna confronted her mom about knowingly selling her into sex slavery. Tears flowed as her mother finally admitted that she had known what she was doing. That however was nothing compared to the emotion displayed when Donna reached deeply into her own renovated heart and forgave her mom for everything she put her through. Fortunately, few of us will ever be called to the level of forgiveness Donna was called to give. I pray I will one day obtain that level of Christlikeness.

Not long after her return to the States, Donna's dad suffered a stroke and was being left by his family to simply die. Thanks to the generosity of our supporters AIM was able to cover the inpatient care her father needed, but no one in their family was willing to care for him once he was discharged from the hospital. Donna was now faced with another difficult choice. While her dad was not actively involved in her trafficking, he was complicit. He was happy to live off the money from the sale of his daughter. Once again, Donna made the choice to forgive and love some one who had forsaken her. But this time her sacrifice was more than emotional and spiritual, it was also material and physical.

Using her savings, Donna flew back to Cambodia, found a tiny house, picked up her dad at the hospital, and they moved in together. For the next six months she provided 24/7 care for her father. This meant she carried him everywhere he needed to go, like to the bathroom. This was no small feat as Donna is less than five feet tall, and weighs less than one hundred pounds. Her dad is bigger. Each day she bathed him, she fed him, and she took him through his much needed physical therapy. Through Donna's loving care her father recovered.

Donna, like Amy, Betty, Carol, and so many others, is an example of a young girl who experienced more trauma than any of us can imagine, and yet has had her heart so fully healed that she pours herself out in love to the people around her.

## Introduction: Slaves Turned Abolitionists

Even to those who hurt her.
Even to the undeserving.
Even when it leads her back into the painful places.
Just as her Savior did.

When people are confronted with the evil of child sex trafficking, far too often they feel overwhelmed with its size and complexity. Thinking they lack what's needed to stand with the oppressed and fight injustice, they choose to look away. In fighting this evil for eighteen years we've learned this just isn't true. We have seen God do so much with the little we have to offer.

We see it in the faces of these beautiful, strong, resilient girls.

We see it in the thousands of staff, volunteers, and donors who have given sacrificially to rescue these girls and provide them a path to becoming everything God has made them to be.

We have learned no one is out of reach, no one is too broken, no one is too insignificant to be used by God for greater things than any of us can imagine. That includes me. It also includes you. You may not feel capable of fighting an evil as dark and widespread as child sex trafficking. I didn't, but God did, and he provided. As we joined with others to obey God's command to stand with the oppressed and fight injustice we experienced victory.

I write this book so you will not feel overwhelmed or hopeless about the instances of oppression and injustice in this world. I write to inspire you to answer God's call for you to join the fight. Some will be called to leave their homes, some will be called to open their homes, some will be called to merely change the way they live in their homes. Whatever our calling, through our unified efforts God will transform individual lives, families, communities, and more.

In the pages ahead, I will dive more deeply into the stories of these and other girls while revealing the incredible things God has done for them and through them. I'll also explain everything that it takes to bring these beautiful young women from slaves to modern-day abolitionists. I'll recount how Bridget and I left our comfortable life in the suburbs to devote ourselves to ending the evils of sex trafficking. I'll share both our successes and failures, as we learn and grow from both. As you read, however, please keep your heart open to what God may be calling you to do.

You will find proof on every page that God does the impossible and reigns as our supreme miracle worker. Doing the impossible doesn't depend

## Introduction: Slaves Turned Abolitionists

on our great strategies, abilities, or self-confidence; it is the tangible proof of our Savior Jesus Christ. Here you will find story after story that confirms Paul's assessment: "Brothers and sisters, think of what you were when you were called. Not many of you were wise by human standards; not many were influential; not many were of noble birth. But God chose the foolish things of the world to shame the wise; God chose the weak things of the world to shame the strong. God chose the lowly things of this world and the despised things—and the things that are not—to nullify the things that are, so that no one may boast before him" (1 Corinthians 1:26–29 NIV).

The power belongs to God. The results are up to God. Our job is simply to say "yes" to his call.

# CHAPTER 1: CAMBODIA

*"I can get you a girl as young as you want."*
—Trafficker in Cambodia

When we first started fighting the trafficking that was taking place in Cambodia (around nineteen years ago), it was shockingly easy for a pedophile to obtain a young girl. The pedophile would come into the country and brazenly ask where they could find a young girl to have sex with. Most were directed to the village of Svay Pak, eleven kilometers north of Phnom Penh. Prior to our move to Cambodia, sexualized little girls were on display for purchase. After our move it was generally believed that child sex trafficking was no longer taking place in Svay Pak, but that was not the case. After the airing of several news documentaries about child sex trafficking in Svay Pak the evil evolved; it was now hidden. More on that later.

Betty, whom you met in the introduction, was one of thousands of sex-trafficked girls in Cambodia. Her mother, the woman who gave birth to her and should have been responsible for her care, development, and flourishing, sold her instead. And sold her in to the most horrifying existence imaginable. Allow the reality of that to sink in for a moment. This is a mother who took her own daughter and willingly placed her in a situation where she would be literally enslaved. This mother put her beautiful child in a brothel, where some of the most depraved men on the planet would routinely abuse her physically, sexually, and emotionally. Five times a day, every day. Terror and abuse for the low price of $20. Betty would kick, scream, cry, and beg to avoid this torture and degradation. Instead of sympathy, she would receive physical blows and verbal abuse from her trafficker: another mother inflicting hell on a young girl.

In exchange for damning her own daughter to this earthly version of hell, Betty's mother received a relatively low sum of money to pay off some debts.

Betty described her feelings as only a girl who has suffered like she has could: "I felt like I was hopeless," she said. "I had nothing. No one cared about me and no one thought I was special. In my future, I thought I would die."

Betty is special and unique, but sadly her story is very common in Cambodia.

Think of all the layers of evil that have to converge to allow a sweet little girl like Betty to be subjected to this hell. Parents are the victims of predatory loans that make them beholden to people who manipulate them as they seek to ease their unbearable impoverished existence. Traffickers create a network and mechanism for buying and transporting young girls to brothels. The traffickers, brothel owners, and their families enslave the girls and facilitate their abuse. Entire villages keep silent about what they know is happening all around them. Police and other authorities either turn a blind eye, or lack the training and support to intercede, or in some cases directly profit from the sale and abuse of these girls. And all of this is fueled by a seemingly unlimited supply of pedophiles—some of whom are Cambodian but most of whom travel from Western countries like the United States. This pedophilia in turn is fueled by the now-dominant porn industry and the witting and unwitting porn users who make it a massive and financially rewarding industry.

It is a concert of evil that ruins lives and constitutes one of Satan's greatest triumphs in all of human history. If you ever want to be reminded about the depths of evil that humanity is capable of, reread the paragraph above. It takes a lot of different people to make the whole operation work, but tragically there is never a shortage of people doing their part to engage in this deep darkness on every level.

Trafficking is a huge problem. But another major aspect of the problem is this: Even as awareness grows very few people are engaging in the fight against this evil. Especially when compared to the numbers involved in perpetrating it! You are clearly a person who cares, otherwise you wouldn't be reading this book. The key as you read is not to be overcome by the size of the problem or the depth of the evil, but to be inspired by the impact the love of a single person can have in defeating evil. As we look at all the factors/people involved in perpetrating evil, we can be led into

## Chapter 1: Cambodia

thinking of macro solutions such as education, economic development, law enforcement, and the justice system. These are good things, they are part of our ministry, but they've never defeated evil. It's love, the love of Jesus that defeats evil, that transforms hearts. And it happens one heart at a time.

Once Bridget and I learned that children like Betty were being abused like this, we knew we had to do something. But the first time we went to Cambodia, we had no idea that this type of evil even existed.

## ADVENTURE

Years before we first arrived in Cambodia, I was a typical American pastor. I had been serving as the executive pastor of Adventure Christian Church in Roseville, California. These were good years. I was happy and fulfilled. Adventure was a lively church that was growing quickly. That's an exciting place to be—you feel like you're doing something right, and it's not hard to see God working during seasons such as these. Like many others, Bridget and I were unaware of the suffering of countless Bettys around the world. But we were about to find out.

Part of my role as the executive pastor was overseeing missions and compassion ministries. So in 2003, Bridget and I decided to take a trip to the Philippines and Cambodia to meet with and encourage some missionaries we had been supporting as a church. We had no idea this trip would change our lives and throw us onto the front lines of a battleground we didn't even known existed.

## THE PHILIPPINES

Our missionaries in the Philippines were running an impressive outreach program to street kids. It was a very different experience for us. The ministry was on the island of Mindanao, a place where the kidnapping of Western visitors was not a rare thing. We had an armed guard with us 24/7—he even slept on the floor outside of our room. To be honest it really wasn't that scary. Our biggest fear was being shot by the guard as we stepped over him to go to the bathroom in the middle of the night. I digress.

This ministry on Mindanao reached out to homeless street kids. Boys and girls who had no future, highly vulnerable children, most physically abused, many sexually abused. These kids were living in great fear. We walked through a fish market and saw these children sleeping on water-soaked concrete, keeping their backs to the wall, just hoping that no one would harm them as they tried to sleep. They were destined for a life where they would never leave the streets. In their hopelessness many turned to huffing glue, the only high they could afford. The ministry reached out to these city kids and offered them a safe home in the mountains, a life-changer for these street kids, as they experienced a loving home for the first time in their lives.

For an American pastor living a comfortable life, an experience like this can have a big impact. It's a life moment all we comfortable American Christians need to experience. And sadly we don't need to leave the United States to experience the desperate need of vulnerable children. After ten days with these kids, we were building relationships. We loved them. Everything in us wanted to stay and be a part of the life transformation of these kids.

In fact, when we boarded the plane from the Philippines to Cambodia, we had a lot on our hearts and minds. We cried on the plane because we already missed the kids and were heartbroken to leave them. We also left with an offer to consider: after our short ten days in the Philippines, the missionaries had asked us to take over the ministry! We obviously weren't expecting this, but somehow, it sounded like a good idea. We were surprised by our own sincerity when we told them we would pray about it. As we traveled from the Philippines to Cambodia, we found that our hearts had already begun to take root in Philippine soil. It would take a lot for Cambodia to even begin to grab our hearts as the Philippines did.

## CAMBODIA

Rather than impressing us and winning our affection, Cambodia made us miss the Philippines. We landed in Phnom Penh, the capital of Cambodia, at night. Even after dark, the climate was hot, sticky, and oppressive. We were uncomfortable from the moment we landed in the ugly Phnom Penh airport. The city reeked with air pollution, and we wished we had never left the mountains of the Philippines. More than that there was an emotional and spiritual darkness that seemed to reach our very souls.

During our ten days in Cambodia, we were constantly on the move, traveling through fourteen provinces in those ten days. This was no easy feat. The roads were still scarred by bombed-out craters. We wondered, how did this happen? Soon we learned of the reign of terror of Pol Pot and

## Chapter 1: Cambodia

the Khmer Rouge. It lasted "only" four years (from 1975 to 1979). There was a brutal civil war leading up to Pol Pot's regime. The devastating effects of his reign and its aftermath continued until 1999, by which time conservative estimates say that two million Cambodians had died as a result of the regime. That's roughly a quarter of Cambodia's population gone, not to mention the social, economic, and governmental collapse. Pol Pot's regime would systematically execute its own people. As his plans to make Cambodia an agrarian utopia failed, he laid blame on the educated, then the religious, and then the family as the foundation of Cambodian society. This led to their execution. In some cases, he had children spy on their parents and report any hint of insurgence. Sometimes these kids-turned-spies would also be forced to take part in the torture and execution of their own parents. There was a depth of depravity in Pol Pot's approach that ate away at the very foundation of Cambodian society. Combined with the abject poverty and corruption today it creates the perfect storm that leads to the sex trafficking of children. It was the cause of the darkness we felt. To understand more fully what happened to Cambodia and America's part in it I highly recommend *Cambodia's Curse: The Modern History of a Troubled Land*, written by Joel Brinkley.

As we drove through this war-scarred country, we had to dodge huge craters caused by land mines, which are still a problem. There's an organization working on finding and removing them, and they say it'll take another fifty years to complete! We did not enjoy ourselves. We traveled from province to province in a twelve-passenger van that typically held twenty people. It seemed we were always driving on those demolished roads. We didn't make nearly enough stops. When Bridget asked to use the bathroom, our driver pulled to the side of the road and told her she could go in the rice paddy just outside of the van. It turns out she couldn't. So out of fear of having to go in front of an audience in an open field, Bridget drank very little water (where was it going to go?), which made her constantly feel ill and dehydrated. She was miserable. Bridget compares the experience of that trip to traveling through one of the rings of hell. We devised a signal that was less than subtle: When Bridget made a siren sound, kind of like the warning for a nuclear disaster, I knew she was about to melt down and needed me to find some way to rescue her.

As we traveled the country, I was speaking to hundreds of Cambodians every day on leadership development. Bridget was working with the kids. These Cambodians were lovely people. They were hungry to learn. I've never seen such aggressive note-taking. They would scribble down everything I said; when they ran out of paper, they'd start taking notes on their arms and legs!

As much as we loved the people, we moved around so much that we didn't have time to build relationships as we had done in the Philippines. Throughout our stay, there was also the weight we felt—spiritually, emotionally, and now physically. During our travels, people would frequently point to huge plots of land and tell us that their family used to live there and work that land before they had been killed or forced to flee by the Khmer Rouge.

Despite this darkness and our inability to connect relationally, the Cambodian people were so generous. Every time we would pull out of a town to move on to the next, adults and children would run behind our van for as long as they were able, waving and smiling. It was beautiful, but also heartbreaking. They sent us home with local clothing, apparently oblivious to the stark reality that we giant Americans would never be able to fit into the beautiful outfits. When we left to get on the plane, they weighed us down with banana chips and all kinds of food because they were afraid we wouldn't be fed on the flight.

As amazing as the people were, the plane trip out of Cambodia was entirely different than the trip out of the Philippines. We cried leaving the Philippines, believing the Lord may have been calling us to that place and those people. We sighed with relief leaving Cambodia, with Bridget affirming for both of us: "Thank God we'll never have to come here again!" We had no sense that there was anything left for us to do in Cambodia.

We had no idea we'd soon see God do the impossible in this hurting country and change our lives in the process.

## CHILDREN FOR SALE

When we returned from our first trip to Cambodia in 2003, even after traveling through so much of the country, we did not have any awareness of the kind of evil that Betty and so many other girls were facing. In our ten days traveling through fourteen provinces, not a single person had ever mentioned human trafficking or the sexual exploitation of women and children. Not once! We felt oppression and grieved for this country, but we didn't have the slightest clue that so many of its young girls were being sold, raped, and destroyed by its own citizens and the rest of the world.

A couple of weeks after we returned from our trip, Bridget was about to turn off the TV and go to bed when a *Dateline* broadcast flashed onto the screen:

"CHILDREN FOR SALE IN CAMBODIA"

We were stunned. The report talked about the enormity of the problem. The Cambodian minister of women's affairs told *Dateline* that an estimated thirty thousand girls had been sex trafficked. They showed hidden camera footage of some of the Americans who came to buy and rape extremely young Cambodian girls. It was overwhelming to watch.

When we sent copies of the broadcast to our connections in Cambodia, they firmly denied that trafficking was happening there. It felt like being in an episode of *The Twilight Zone*. A short time later, however, they called us back and apologized. They had watched the broadcast several times and acknowledged that the problem was real.

We firmly believe that God placed that broadcast in our path for us to do something. At that time we didn't know what we were to do, but felt sure God would make it clear to us. Unbelievably, this moment that felt so personal to us was also a moment in history which would impact the lives of hundreds of girls like Betty! But that's getting ahead of the story.

Now we needed to discover what God was calling us to do, and what it would cost.

# CHAPTER 2: THE DECISION

HAVING FACED THE REALITY that young girls were being trafficked in Cambodia, we began exploring what our California church could do to address the issue. Within six months we had put together another team to head back to Cambodia . . . so much for never going back! We didn't know what was needed, but we were determined to bring the resources of the church to the fight. Our team consisted of therapists, teachers, pastors, educators, and other people we thought could have significance in the fight by approaching the issue from different angles.

Having no idea what to do or how to proceed, we met with NGOs and Cambodian government officials. We felt we needed to better understand how the issue was being addressed and what could be done to end the trafficking of these girls. We quickly learned that the greatest need was aftercare. Simply stated, aftercare is providing a safe home for the rescued victims of child sex trafficking, where they can find healing and be equipped to safely return to Cambodian society.

We found out that organizations such as International Justice Mission (IJM) had been doing the important work of rescuing girls from brothels. Unfortunately, IJM had paused rescue efforts because there was nowhere for these girls to go, aftercare being almost nonexistent. Physically rescued, the girls would end up back in the brothels, with a deeper sense of hopelessness. It seemed if we wanted to be part of the solution, we would need to create a place for rescued girls to go, be cared for, and find healing. So we explored what this would entail. Our meetings were extremely encouraging, each one confirming the call God had placed on our hearts to fight for the freedom of these children. We had just one more meeting; it was the following day. We decided to visit the village of Svay Pak.

Chapter 2: The Decision

## WALKING INTO SVAY PAK

Svay Pak is a little village just eleven kilometers north of Phnom Penh. Trash and other waste was scattered on streets of mud. The smell of cooking fires and human waste filled the air. Random utility lines intersected overhead like a giant spider's web. We had learned that this place was infamous in the world of human trafficking and child sex tourism. Specifically, this little village was known as the place to buy extremely young girls, as young as five years old, to be used for sexual exploitation. Simply put, a haven for pedophiles. Men traveled from around the globe to buy children in this village.

We hoped by visiting this village we could gain insight into the evil we were about to fight. So we went to Svay Pak. Our first glimpse of this village and our first attempt at walking down the street where children were sold was in the middle of the afternoon. Even then, Bridget couldn't walk down the street with us; our Cambodian guide told us it was too dangerous. I continued on with a couple of the men on our team. We hadn't taken more than a few steps into the village when we started getting negative attention. The villagers were used to foreign visitors, including American men. But the American men they were used to were sex tourists, and those men didn't want to draw attention to themselves. By contrast, we came walking down the street carrying a camera to document everything we were seeing. I know you must be thinking that was naive or even stupid. You are right, it was.

It became immediately obvious that the villagers were not going to allow us to look around. A number of men physically blocked our path while yelling at the top of their lungs. We quickly turned back with nothing more than the obvious impression there was something going on that they didn't want us to see. In the future we would return with a much better plan.

## THE LAST MEETING

Our last meeting was with a large ministry that was just beginning to provide aftercare for rescued victims of child sex trafficking. A member of our church had used his influence to set up a meeting with the country director. We were escorted to a conference room and waited with high expectations for his arrival. To say that our meeting was discouraging is a major understatement.

It was less like a meeting, more like an interrogation. After questioning our qualifications (we had none), he concluded with the following statement: "Go back home, send money, and let the big dogs do the work."

I was devastated! I even began to question God's calling. It is sad that one negative meeting can somehow overshadow twelve encouraging meetings, and how it led me to forget the months of prayer and the confirmation received from godly men and women. The country director was right, we weren't qualified—heck, we didn't even have a plan. However, the Bible is full of God using those who the world sees as unqualified. As someone once said, "God doesn't call the qualified, he qualifies the called." Once God reminded us of this truth, Bridget's and my heart were filled with a passion to help the child victims of sex trafficking in Cambodia by opening a home for those rescued. But we still didn't think it meant moving there.

## MOVING TO CAMBODIA

When we got back home from that second trip to Cambodia and were processing everything we had learned and seen, we knew we couldn't follow the advice we had received to simply stay home and send money. We decided we had to send some people over there. We figured that we could find the right people to contribute their time, expertise, and finances to the fight against trafficking in unique ways. Other groups we talked with hadn't yet developed a complete plan of care for helping rescued girls either, so we got to work creating our own. We ended up developing an eighty-page document with the help of professional therapists, social workers, and psychologists. It outlined a plan of care to bring healing and restoration to the rescued victims.

We were sure someone from our church would accept the challenge and get to work in Cambodia, someone other than Bridget and me.

I stood in front of our church, which had now grown to over seven thousand people attending each weekend, and laid out the problem as compellingly as I could. I was specific with the needs and explicit in calling for some people in our midst to accept the challenge and move to Cambodia. We knew we had a good base of people who were devoted to following God's leading, so we were confident that God would nudge the right people to take a step of faith.

Our action point from that sermon was to come to an informational meeting. Out of seven thousand people, about three hundred showed up

## Chapter 2: The Decision

to learn more about the problem. We were confident there was someone in the three hundred God was calling to Cambodia. Again we were specific. Again I thought we were compelling. Everything went great and people were genuinely moved. But when the night ended and we checked the sign-up sheets to see who was interested in potentially moving, there was not a single name. The only people left standing there at the end of the night were Bridget and me.

Bridget turned to me and said, "It can't be us, can it?"

We took all of this to prayer. We genuinely did not know what the Lord had in store. Bridget and I decided to spend a day in a retreat. We wouldn't interact with each other all day—never mind that it happened to be our fourteen-year anniversary—and then at the end of the day we would meet to discuss what the Lord was impressing on us. That's how we found ourselves sitting across from each other at an Italian restaurant at the end of a prayer-filled day in December 2004, about to make one of the biggest decisions of our lives. We decided to do a countdown and simultaneously reveal what God had said to us:

One, two, three . . .

"It's us."

We both said it at exactly the same moment. Neither of us felt any doubt that this was what we should do. I had actually gotten excited about the possibility of seeing God work like this. Bridget told me that the more she looked up the atrocities of Pol Pot and the Khmer Rouge, the more she looked at pictures of the Cambodian people, looking directly into their eyes, the less she was able to resist. She said, "If this were me, and I had lost my kids, I would need someone to help me. Now that we know what we know, I would be so ashamed to stand before the Lord and say I didn't help."

We knew what we had to do. This realization began our journey of starting Agape International Missions' anti-trafficking work. We knew we were opening a home for rescued victims. We had no idea how hard it would be or how deeply our hearts would break. We had no idea the extent of the hell that these little girls were forced to endure.

But, we also had no idea how powerful the gospel of Jesus really is, though we had believed it and taught it for years. We had no idea how fully God can transform a life that has been trampled and discarded. We had no idea what it would be like to watch God use his Church to transform a village and even the lives of people who were being used by Satan to perpetrate the greatest evil of our lifetimes.

## A LESSON LEARNED

As I wrote above, there was a short time I questioned God's call on my life, in spite of the hours of prayer and the confirmation of godly people who we knew well and trusted fully. While I think it is important to confirm God's call, once it's confirmed, we must not let others' or Satan's road blocks stop us. We must anticipate them when following Jesus and persevere to overcome them. The Bible is clear that following Jesus will not be easy.

We have a dear friend, Jessica Munoz, who was given the vision of an aftercare home for the rescued victims of child sex trafficking in Hawaii. There were many obstacles for her to overcome to see this vision realized. So many obstacles that it took her fifteen years to see the vision become a reality! Today, her organization, Hoʻōla Nā Pua, has that aftercare home where children are experiencing the love of Jesus and finding healing. Those committed to standing with the oppressed and fighting injustice are fueled to persevere by our love and encouragement.

Bridget and I have been loved and encouraged by literally thousands of staff, volunteers, and supporters. We have been, and are, incredibly blessed.

Please consider how you can love and encourage someone standing with the oppressed and fighting injustice. Most times it requires little effort, and the results can be transformative.

# CHAPTER 3: WHO'S ON OUR TEAM?

## SETTING THE TARGET

It was clear from our meetings in Cambodia that an aftercare home for the rescued victims was the most urgent need. There were teams in place to conduct the rescues, but the missing piece was a home where they could send the survivors. The hopelessness felt by victims is only confirmed as they return to the very lives they were saved from. A rescue without healing is worse than no rescue at all.

Think about the harsh realities these very young girls face. They have been raised in extreme poverty and then sold, usually by a family member for labor or sex, as early as five years old. They have been taught by their families, their traffickers, and their abusers that they are worthless, that they will never amount to anything, that their life of being forced to gratify the depraved desires of men is the only life they can expect.

The hopelessness they feel is reinforced by the culture in which they live. A familiar Cambodian proverb reads, "Boys are like gold, girls are like white linen." It is interpreted by the culture to mean, like gold, nothing done to a boy reduces his value; however, once a girl loses her virginity, like soiled white linen, she no longer has value. Grant a girl like that her freedom, one who sees herself as having no value in her own eyes and in the eyes of her society, set her loose on the street, and what do you expect her to make of herself?

## MAKING A PLAN

It was only after we had decided to provide an aftercare home for these girls that we asked ourselves the question, "How?" The answer was way out of our league. How would we care for girls that have been rescued out of such horrific abuse? What care could we offer that would restore their shattered bodies and souls and make them fruitful members of society? The more we talked to groups on the ground in Cambodia, the more we realized that nobody had a proven plan for us to follow. We would learn from each other.

We worked hard with our group of therapists, psychologists, social workers, pastors, teachers, and a few others to develop something we felt was holistic. We ended up with a forty-page plan of care that detailed the policies and procedures we would follow. It involved meeting five areas of essential needs: physical, psychosocial, educational, spiritual, and successful reintegration. It was a good plan, but the details often changed based on the experiences of both our successes and failures. God blessed AIM with a gifted staff to work alongside us and implement the change needed to build a transformational program.

Once Bridget and I realized we were the ones God was calling to go to Cambodia, we began writing our personal five-year plan for launching the program for our aftercare home. This was how long we thought it would take to hire and train the local staff, and fill the facility with rescued girls. At the end of that five-year plan, Bridget and I would lovingly pass on the ministry to the local Cambodian staff and then fly safely back to California to resume our pastoral ministry at the same church.

We were developing what we thought was all God had for us to do in Cambodia, including details and timelines. It was such a good plan! I'm sure God was smiling at our naive attempts at responsible planning.

We decided we would train the local staff for a full year before we opened the facility. As you can imagine, this was a difficult decision, because there were so many girls that needed help immediately. However, we had seen what happened to these girls when well-intentioned groups jumped into action without a comprehensive plan and without proper training. Looking back, the plan to train staff for a full year was a wise decision.

We have seen so many hearts and lives transformed through the love that rescued girls have received in our aftercare homes. This doesn't happen by accident. It takes amazingly patient, gracious, and loving people to care for these girls. Our staff puts up with a shocking amount of defiance, disrespect, and nastiness from many of the girls when they first enter our

## Chapter 3: Who's on Our Team?

homes. While that's understandable given what these girls have endured, it still takes a special person to respond with unconditional love and patience while waiting for the heart transformation God wants for each child.

## OUR VANISHING BASE

While our staff needed this extensive level of training, we took a lot of criticism for our slow approach. Many people, pastors, and churches back in the United States were helping to fund our efforts, and it was hard for them to see things move so slowly. *Where were the girls we were supposed to be caring for? What did we have to show for the money they had been sending us?*

But the criticism didn't stop there. We rented a house in Cambodia that allowed us to shelter and care for the girls. Some were upset about our selection, saying that the house we had picked for the girls was too nice for them.

At the same time, we had also been discovering that it's far easier to write a plan of care than it is to implement it. From the very beginning of our year-long launch, we realized that finding staff to train would be difficult. *Where does a person find staff for this kind of endeavor?*

There was literally no one with the needed experience, including ourselves! In addition to this, we had learned enough about the dynamics in Cambodia to know that we needed to hire both Cambodian and Vietnamese staff. Sadly, racism exists around the world in many forms. The girls we would be caring for would certainly come from both Vietnamese and Cambodian families. There is a shocking amount of racism, prejudice, and animosity between these two. While we were prepared for this reality, we had no idea how deep these prejudices would run and how difficult they would be to overcome. We soon found that job skills, policies, and procedures were easy to train compared to the reconciliation we needed to facilitate between our Cambodian and Vietnamese staff.

Without a single help-wanted listing, based solely on word of mouth, God provided the right people. People with both the heart and experience the girls needed. We in turn invested ourselves into the difficulties of building and training our staff that first year. It seemed God was meeting all our needs, but an email we received just as we prepared to open the home took away that feeling of progress.

Our home church had committed a gift of $250,000. It took us by surprise when we received an email that they would not be able to keep their commitment. *What?! What was happening to our five-year plan?!*

Bridget and I suspected that this was the end of our fight against trafficking. We had sold our home and moved around the world to answer God's call, and now we would have to shut down before we even opened our doors. Without question, if the church had not promised us that money, we would have delayed our move. We didn't know what to do, so we started talking about traveling back to the United States to try to raise funds.

A week or two later my phone started ringing at 3 AM. This is an unfortunate side effect of living across the world from friends and family. It was our friend, John, calling to ask if there was someone who could come and pick up a check to help fund our efforts. This was very sweet, we were thankful that God was making small movements to show us that he would still provide for us. When we found a tactful way to ask John how much the check was made out for, he said: "$250,000."

We were speechless. John was a member of our home church, but he had no idea the church had been unable to keep their financial commitment to us.

This was not the last time that God would provide for our needs or show us that we didn't need to understand how he would do it. The reality is, God's plan has always been better than any planning we have done. We have rarely known in advance what he would do or how he would do it. But God has always been so faithful to our work. Simply put, the plans we have made over the years have proven to be extremely unimpressive when we consider them next to the reality of what God has unfolded year after year.

## INCHING FORWARD

Our plodding obedience to God has been a process of learning to trust, and of discovering time and again that God knows better than anyone else. He knows better than we do when we try to plan out what type of impact we'd like to have, and he knows better than the so-called "experts."

I will never forget that we were told by one of the "experts" not to come to Cambodia. It would be better for us to simply send our money because they were already doing everything that could be done. As God would have it, we eventually found ourselves in a situation where our aftercare home was located next door to theirs. For a period of time, our facility shared a wall with them. The girls in our home would shout over the wall to girls under their care. Girls from their home would climb over the wall to get into ours. It seemed their home had either too many girls, or not enough staff.

The day came when they asked us to take a few girls from their home, those they found too difficult to handle. Betty was one of them. We immediately agreed. It wasn't long after their home was closed, and we took in the rest of the girls who remained there.

I was hesitant to share this story because it could come across as prideful. There was a time it gave me a little unhealthy pride, resulting in a happy, "we won" attitude. We're the best! Thankfully God did not let the prideful feeling last long, at least it didn't seem long from my perspective. What God showed me was the obvious truth: everyone lost when the home closed as now there were fewer places for the rescued child victims who so desperately needed a loving home to bring them healing.

## WHO ARE WE LISTENING TO

I share this story to illustrate one thing: Be careful who you listen to.

First and foremost, we have to listen to God rather than human beings, even the experts. If we had listened to the experts, the girls in our aftercare home would have ended up back on the street, or maybe never rescued at all. God had us there in the right place at the right time. And if we had listened to the experts, then none of the two thousand-plus girls who have been rescued through AIM's efforts at the time I'm writing this would have been rescued, healed, and successfully reintegrated into Cambodian society.

Second, I suggest we use great caution when listening to experts who think they have nothing to learn from those seeking their advice. My experience is that pride has hardened their hearts. All of us can learn every day from every person we are in contact with.

Finally, no matter how much expertise and or success we may have, we must always be active and sincere listeners to those who have less expertise than us, even those with none. So if you have an idea, or a thought on how we can better stand with the oppressed and fight injustice please email me at donb@aimfree.org and we'll start a conversation.

# CHAPTER 4: PRINCESSES

When a girl has been rescued from a brothel there are at least four thing she believes for certain:

(1) No one loves me.

(2) No one can be trusted.

(3) Everyone will use me.

(4) There is no hope for me.

We have never had a girl enter our aftercare home who didn't deeply believe these four things. Why? Because up to the point of rescue in their lives, they believe, and for good reason, everyone they have ever met has worked diligently together to prove those four things true, again and again.

The question is, "How do we begin to change these beliefs?" Each one of us, not just the girls, needs the opposite of these four beliefs in order to survive. We need someone who loves us. We need someone we can trust. We need someone who will do the best for us. We need someone to give us hope. Jesus is the one person who can deliver on all these needs, but he doesn't do it directly. He does it through us, his followers.

The process of experiencing Jesus and his love takes time. We needed something to begin the process. Our consulting psychologist and board member, Dr. Becca Johnson, had a wonderful idea.

## THE PRINCESS PARTY

When a girl enters our aftercare home, she gets a tour of the place, meets the other girls and our staff, and sits through an orientation where we explain her rights, responsibilities, and procedures that are designed to protect the girls and provide a pathway to a new way of living. All of this is

## Chapter 4: Princesses

good and necessary, but none of it changes the girls' beliefs. The four core beliefs remain.

But every time we bring new girls into the home, we now end their first day with an event that cracks open the door to a change in beliefs and true healing. We call it the Princess Party.

After all of the paperwork is done and the girls have met their counselors, house moms, and the other girls living in their home, we bring them into the dining hall. The first thing each girl sees when she enters the room is a poster with her face on it (we take their photo during the intake process) and a heading that reads, for example, "Betty is a princess." (Each girl gets her own poster.) Once the girls are in the room, we begin the ceremony by singing worship songs. The new girls sit and watch while the other girls who have lived in the home sing.

Then our spiritual formation director explains that a princess is the daughter of the King. The director opens their Bible and explains that God is the one true King and that each of us is a son or a daughter of God. So, in fact, they are princesses. Then the director invites the new princesses to come forward. They are usually timid, at first, because they don't know what is going to happen.

Remember that these girls are newly rescued children. For many of them, this is literally the first day, in a long time, that they haven't been raped multiple times.

As these children of God reach the front of the room, all of the other girls and staff begin cheering for them. Each girl is presented with her poster and told, "This is a reminder of who you truly are. You are God's daughter. You are a princess. This is how we see you: as a princess."

At this point in the ceremony, each girl's house mom comes forward and places a crown on her head. The crown itself isn't valuable; it's plastic with a few glass jewels, but what it represents is priceless. All of the girls cheer once again and then we throw a party in honor of the new princesses. The girls get to enjoy soft drinks and snacks while our friendliest girls intentionally befriend the newcomers, their new sisters.

As I describe the Princess Party, it doesn't sound like much. It doesn't cost very much, it doesn't last very long, and all of it can appear to be a little cheesy. I have seen *a lot* of these ceremonies and they never get old. There is such great power in each moment. To these children, it's a *huge* deal. For these children, fresh out of the hellish depths of human trafficking, the princess experience is jarring. No one has ever celebrated these cherished children of God. No one has ever cheered for them. No one has ever told them that they are special.

Prior to the Princess Party, every time one of these girls had been singled out it's either because they were being punished or were being forced into having sex with a stranger (raped). But, at our aftercare home, they are being addressed and celebrated for a simple reason: God loves them and we love them.

We started the Princess Parties because we thought it would be a special moment, but we had no idea how big of an impact this would have on the girls. The girls have huge, beautiful smiles. Often, they are beaming as their new family applauds for them. In Cambodian culture, being a princess is a big deal. There is still a royal family in Cambodia, and although their role is purely symbolic in modern politics, the king, princes, and princesses receive tremendous respect and admiration from the Cambodian people. Each girl wonders, "Could it be that I will be respected and admired?"

## CHANGING BELIEFS

Betty, whose story you heard in the introduction, came to us in the early days of launching our aftercare home. She was exactly the kind of girl we were praying to be able to help when we moved to Cambodia. Having grown up in extreme poverty, sold into sex slavery by her own mother, held captive in a brothel where she was pimped out five times a day, few could have reasonably expected Betty to find substantial healing for the physical, emotional, and psychological abuse she had endured.

When she was rescued from the brothel she was being held in, the worst part of her personal hell was over. But she was still far from a storybook ending.

Immediately after her rescue, Betty was taken to an aftercare facility that was funded by the government of Finland. Before long, however, they cut off the funding. Without money to pay anyone, the facility shut down within a week. Though she had been pulled out of the brothel, Betty was not gaining trust in her new situation.

Betty and the other girls were passed on to another aftercare home. They did their best to care for her, but Betty was tough. Really tough! In order to survive as a sex slave she lied, was manipulative, self-centered, and disrespected authority. Her initial experience in aftercare homes reinforced her belief that these traits were the means of her survival. Betty was one of

## Chapter 4: Princesses

their most difficult cases. In time, this group decided that they weren't able to care for her.

Ever since we started our aftercare home in Phnom Penh, Bridget and I had consistently prayed, *"Lord, bring us the most difficult cases."*

We decided that we hadn't given up our old lives and moved across the world to do what came the easiest. We had planned to enter hell and, through the power of God's unconditional love, bring healing to places and people who seemed irreparably damaged. We sincerely wanted to care for the girls who were hurting the most because we believe that God can heal more than we dare to hope.

The director of Betty's second aftercare home knew that we had been praying this way, so he asked if we would be willing to take a group of ten or twelve girls—including Betty—who were proving too difficult for them. We were thrilled to have the opportunity to help, so we enthusiastically welcomed her and the other girls into our aftercare home.

What Betty had been through up until the point when she walked into our home is far beyond most of our worst nightmares. Sold by her mom, beaten and threatened, and pimped out by the woman who imprisoned her. Raped by countless Westerners. Passed on by the people who initially rescued her. For her first three years with us I had my own nickname for Betty, PITA. Not the Middle Eastern bread, it was an acronym for pain in the ass. Of course she was. Should we expected her to act any other way after experiencing a childhood of unending pain? Everyone she had ever known had betrayed her and subjected her to a living hell. Why should she assume that we would be any different? We told her she was loved, and that she was special. Our staff was now about to love and care for her in a way that would prove it was true!

## PERSEVERING LOVE IN ACTION

Betty's story is a testimony to the power of unconditional love. At the aftercare home, the girls are clustered into groups with "house moms" caring for their girls. Because of this setup, the house moms were the ones who experienced Betty at her absolute worst. But they kept on loving her, no matter how awful she was to them. They could see something of value in her. These moms would never have tolerated her behavior from their own children, but they knew how much Betty needed their grace and persistent love.

Betty now talks about how much encouragement she received from all of us during those years: "They always tell me that I am special" she said, "Especially Don. He always says that I'm special. Before I could not get it because I thought I was not special, but he always says it and now I know I'm special."

The thing is, out of everyone who interacted with her during those years, I was certainly the worst at loving her. Bridget and the house moms were a hundred times better than I was. But I was the first man who had ever treated Betty like a daughter. She's right that I kept telling her that she was special. I believed it, so I said it constantly. This is the power of persistent love. Even though I told Betty she was special, it was through God that she became special in her own eyes.

As we continued to show Betty unconditional love, we also taught her about Jesus, as we do with all of the girls. We have never forced any of the girls to listen or respond, but we believe that unconditional love cannot be fully understood without understanding Jesus. Because of this, we believe that presenting the girls with the unconditional love of Jesus is essential to the healing process. They choose on their own to take it or leave it, and girls do experience substantial healing even if they don't believe as we do.

But as Jesus said, "No one has greater love than this: to lay down his life for his friends" (John 15:13). Not only did Jesus say that, he also did it. There is no better way to demonstrate to these girls—or to anyone—what redemptive love looks like.

It became Betty's understanding that the love she received from the staff, the love that began her heart transformation, was from Jesus. It was seeing and experiencing that same unconditional, self-sacrificing love reflected in the house moms that helped her internalize the fact that she was worthy of love. It was through the perseverance of this loving family, that over time, Betty found herself prepared to carry that same love to other girls in need.

## ABOUT PERSEVERING LOVE

Personally, I believe the unconditional love these girls need in order to move from victim, to survivor, to thriving is beyond our human capacity. It's only when we become conduits of Jesus' love that the healing miracles take place. There were days when my human love would run out at about 9 AM. Actually, that was most days. It was only when I was connected to Jesus that love for others flowed all day long. Whatever it takes to stay connected to Jesus has to be our top priority.

Finally, you may be wondering what heart-transforming love looks like. You may be disappointed. It's quite pedestrian. It's made up of simple acts that continue regardless of the responses they engender. Here's a brief list of some of the things our staff does to love the girls:

- Carefully prepare and serve meals, with second helpings.
- Play games.
- Listening without judging or fixing.
- Give encouraging words.
- Help in discovering gifts and talents, and help in developing them.
- Help in discovering life dreams and navigating them.
- Recognizing even the smallest improvement and celebrating it.
- Correcting in love, not in anger.
- Give a desired, but unearned gift.
- Saying thank you to a girl who was only doing what she was expected to do.
- Dry their tears and joyfully laugh with them.

Gosh, I feel loved by the same things. How about you? Do you know anyone who needs that kind of love today?

# CHAPTER 5: LESSONS IN LOVE

When I was a child, my birth mom was abusive to me. By the time I turned five, my parents divorced and I went with my dad to live with my grandparents in their very small house. They attended church and took me along every Sunday. At the time I considered church an unwanted interruption; it would take almost thirty years before I felt otherwise. But that's another story.

This story is about the greatest example of unconditional love I know of outside of Jesus.

My dad and stepmom always loved me, and were incredibly good to me. I loved them dearly. But it was my grandparents who spent the most time with me, who I loved the most, and who would become my heroes by their extraordinary example of love. Especially my grandpa. I called him Pa.

He was kind to everyone he met, always made time for people. He grew up poor, yet instead of clinging to what he earned, over time he gave away everything.

Pa worked well into his eighties, right up until the day he died. I remember him working in a shoe factory, then later in a grocery store, packing bags. His last job was as a crossing guard, helping kids cross the street into a park. There was one mentally handicapped adult named Joe who would always visit the park, and my grandfather would help him cross the street. Eventually, Joe wouldn't go into the park, but would just hang out with Pa. Pa being who he was started to bring a chair for Joe so he didn't have to stand or sit on the ground. Before long he started bringing Joe lunch.

Pa worked as a crossing guard from 9 am to 9 pm. The work wasn't too taxing, but still that's a long time for a man in his eighties to be working! Toward the end of the day, I would go out for a run and bring him a drink along the way. One day as I ran up to bring him his Coke, I saw a bunch

## Chapter 5: Lessons in Love

of police cars and ambulances, lights flashing. My first thought was a kid got hit by a car, and I was worried about how hard that would be on my grandfather.

As I got closer, Joe came up to me and told me, "They took your grandpa. He's gone to the hospital." I ran to the nearby hospital and found my Pa in the ER. He was covered in his own blood with tubes running everywhere. My eyes welled with tears. I'm sure I had a terrified look on my face when Pa raised his trembling hand, placed it on mine, and said, "Don't worry, I love you." A few minutes later he died.

What?! How could this be?! I couldn't understand how Pa suffering so much, yet worried about me, still conveyed his love for me. I remember thinking, "If I can just be a little bit like Pa I'll be okay."

It wasn't until later that I connected his selflessness to his faith in Jesus.

Years later, when I was going through a divorce, a man that I worked with named Don invited me to his house. It was a simple act of love, but he began inviting me to spend time with him and his family. I was not the type of guy you asked to spend time with your family. I was the type of guy you invite to wild parties, with no kids.

Somehow Don could see through my party guy exterior where within lay a broken heart. Once again it was a Christian who was loving me at another incredibly low point in my life. The love I experienced through Don and his family was transformational. It led me back to church.

Through people like Don and Pa, I was experiencing the love of Jesus. At church I learned that Jesus was the ultimate example and source of unconditional love. Though I, like every human being, had rebelled against God's good design and rule over the world. The only thing that was keeping me away from the restoration that my soul needed was my own refusal to let go of my sin. I learned that rather than trying to work things out for myself, I needed to embrace Jesus, who gave his life so that I could find forgiveness, healing, and a restored relationship with God. When I was drawn to the selfless love of Don and Pa, I was getting a glimpse of the kind of love Jesus offers every human being. I began to recognize that the reason why these two men were able to love me so deeply in my lowest moments was because they had experienced the love of Jesus.

These realizations changed my life because they opened me to directly experiencing the love of Jesus. That love has never stopped transforming my life and calling me into situations where I have the privilege of being a conduit of Jesus' love. Since moving to Cambodia, I have seen that same love that has been transforming my life work miracles in the girls that God has brought to our ministries.

## LEARNING TO MEET NEEDS

Before we moved to Cambodia, we worked with therapists in the United States to develop our approach to caring for girls rescued from trafficking and sex slavery. We wanted to make sure that God's love would be present in everything we did and made practical to the real needs of the girls.

From the very beginning, we have utilized trauma focused cognitive behavioral therapy (TF-CBT). This approach to therapy wasn't developed as an intentional Bible-based therapy, but we immediately recognized how many key biblical insights shine through as the healing process unfolds.

There are many steps along the path to recovery. The Princess Party is important in the psychosocial healing process as the girls begin to see themselves differently and are given the opportunity to reclaim the way they understand themselves with regard to the people and the society around them.

Bridget and I didn't have the knowledge or background to know TF-CBT or Princess Parties. Once again God provided. He sent our way Dr. Becca Johnson, a clinical psychologist who specializes in working with trauma victims. She took the TF-CBT therapy and made some adjustments so it would better fit the Cambodian context. She then trained our counselors and set up our therapy process. She also introduced us to Princess Parties. God, as always, provided for us the very best. Dr. Becca is recognized worldwide as an expert in treating traumatized children. Today she continues to periodically train our staff, is an active of the AIM board, and trains organizations around the globe in caring for traumatized children.

We learned that another stage in this process would be helping the girls find healing with regard to their families, most of whom had played a large and typically active role in them being sold into slavery.

One of the major chains that keeps the girls enslaved is the lie that they owe their entire lives to their families. Even when we physically free a girl, she can't heal or mentally break free from the world of sex slavery until she breaks free from that lie. Many of these girls have been told that they are responsible for keeping their families afloat financially, and being sold is the only means they have of doing that.

## Chapter 5: Lessons in Love

Through therapy and education, with God's help, we can replace lies with truth. However, that is a process that takes time. In order to kick start the process we began to give small business loans to these girls' families. We would also offer business training for whatever business venture in which they wanted to engage. The girls would come with us so that they could see that their family's needs were taken care of. In all honesty, for a variety of reasons, these loans typically didn't work out in terms of businesses for these families. But we would give these families the opportunity to earn money, other than by prostituting their daughters. This allowed the process of healing to begin as the girls could see their families didn't have to sell them.

Another important step in healing is to give and receive love in healthy ways. We have a larger gathering area in our aftercare home where we do devotions and teach the girls about the love of Jesus. In that space, we keep a collection box for the poor. (The girls are given opportunities to earn small stipends that are theirs to use as they please.) Giving is anonymous: no one knows who has given, or who hasn't given. It's always surprising how much has been donated at the end of the month. We use the money to buy big bags of rice for a school and orphanage located at the city dump. The girls hand out the food themselves. At Christmas we take the girls to that dump to do an outreach for the children living there. They give little presents they've made and lead the kids in arts and crafts. This dynamic helps the girls learn to love other people in need. The girls in our aftercare homes may have greater needs than those they serve, but it should not blind them to the needs of others. As they begin to heal, they realize that loving and serving others is part of their own healing and the path to an abundant life.

We work hard to provide our girls with an excellent education tailored to their wants and needs. We provide academic, vocational, and life skills training, as well as training in the arts. Our girls are provided with therapy the experts consider the best for those overcoming their trauma resulting from multiple occasions of sexual abuse. But the truth is, I don't think education or therapy has ever healed anyone. That's not to disparage education or therapy. Education gives them a perspective and provides opportunities. Therapy produces survivors who learn to handle life based on everything they've learned. These victims who come out of such hellish circumstances believe that they are trash. They are taught through the events of their lives that they are worthless. They can see clearly that they haven't been loved. In therapy, the counselors and social workers help them learn that they have value. For the first time in their lives, the girls are taught that they are lovable. That's a cognitive understanding that can lead to surviving; however, we and God want them to be thriving.

Thriving happens when these girls actually experience being valued, when they experience unconditional love. This is especially true when they are valued and loved regardless of their behavior. And that happens through the house moms. The counselors and social workers get lifted onto a pedestal because of their professional training, and they play a crucial role. But most of the healing comes as these girls experience the love of God through their house moms. Often the girls will exhibit terrible behavior. And I mean terrible. We don't fault the girls for this because we understand the impact of everything they've been through. Objectively, our girls exhibit behavior that the house moms would never tolerate from their own kids. But the level of patience these house moms maintain is supernatural. They stand there day after day as living proof that the unconditional love of God is real. They pray with the girls and do devotions with them before they go to bed. When they wake up the moms are a reminder that God's love is waiting to carry them through the day. It is absolutely beautiful and an overwhelming reminder every day of how the love of God demonstrated in the selfless love of Jesus changes everything.

To help the girls prepare for what is waiting for them in society, we do role-play in a group therapy setting. We start with really simple things. For example, propose the following situation: "Two of you are in a market and there's one hair ribbon and you both want it. What do you do?"

From there, we advance to more difficult and triggering situations: "You are in a market and someone says, 'You're a whore! I remember you from the brothel.' How do you respond?"

We recognize how difficult this is for the girls but these are real situations that they will undoubtably face when they reenter society. Everyone in their villages know where these girls have been. Often the communication is unspoken. Whether it be a look or simply the way a girl is treated in a specific setting, people in the community have a way of making it loud and clear, without saying a word, that they know these girls have been trafficked and convey their belief that these girls should somehow feel shame for what they've experienced. Again: In Cambodia, boys are gold, girls are cloth.

The healing these girls experience in our aftercare home helps them to believe a simple statement: "I am not who my parents thought I was. I am

## CHAPTER 5: LESSONS IN LOVE

not who the traffickers or Johns thought I was. That's not me, and during that entire time, God never once saw me like that."

Through the hard work of our therapists and social workers, the unconditional love of our house moms, and the healing power of Jesus, these girls have their self-understanding transformed. As we'll see in a later chapter, the girls who go on to reenter Cambodian society with good jobs are able to support themselves and find healthy ways to help their families. When this happens the stigma of their past is replaced by honor in their communities.

## MORE THAN WE CAN HANDLE

A trauma-induced intellectual disability makes life more difficult anywhere, but in Cambodia it can make life impossible. There it is considered a curse from the gods, beyond redemption. It puts an X on your back, making you the target of either neglect or abuse. Because of her intellectual disability Addison was born with that target. To make matters worse, Addison was a girl.

From a very young age, being raped was a consistent part of Addison's life. She was raped by many people in her village, including her own family members. At age twelve, she became pregnant and gave birth to a boy. Her family took in Addison's son, but unbelievably, they kicked her out of the house. Boys are gold and girls are cloth.

Addison did her best to survive on the streets with no resources and no one looking out for her on any level. It didn't go well. One day one of our church members found Addison lying on the street, basically catatonic. Not knowing what to do, but unable to simply walk by without trying to help, this church member brought Addison to our aftercare home.

We could tell immediately that Addison's needs were beyond the level of care our staff, therapists, and house moms could provide. We took her to a psychiatrist to see what could be done for her. The doctor made an evaluation, put Addison on some medication, and placed her in his inpatient clinic. Our staff visited daily. But even with inpatient care and the aid of medication, Addison remained completely nonverbal. Not only was she unable to speak with any of us, she couldn't do even the most basic things necessary to care for herself. The doctor came to the conclusion Addison was beyond hope and discharged her into our care. Despite the complete hopelessness of the situation, our house moms continued loving and caring for Addison, undeterred by the total lack of response.

It became obvious that a house mom caring for Addison along with four or five other girls was not helping. It was extremely difficult for the house mom to manage the responsibility. We needed to develop an individual plan for Addison.

*What if we designated an especially patient house mom to work one-on-one with her everyday?* She would need to love Addison by speaking to someone who never responded. Teaching her to eat, when it meant mostly cleaning up her mess. Potty training a thirteen year old, who had more failures than successes. Playing catch, a form of physical therapy, with someone who never caught or threw. This house mom would need to unconditionally love someone who would never say thanks.

House mom Srey Im was asked to take on this task, and immediately said yes.

This is an important question that has been at the center of everything we have done in Cambodia: *What do you do when it seems there's nothing you can do?* Our answer has consistently been: *Love persistently and unconditionally.*

Love may not seem like much in light of all of the trauma these girls have experienced. It may seem unimpressive next to the advances in medicine and therapy we now have available. We take advantage of those advancements, but over and over again we have encountered proof that unconditional love is the most powerful thing we have to offer.

It took months, and at times it was sad to watch, but eventually Addison began responding to Srey Im and her persevering love. She eventually ate on her own, no longer needed potty training, could play catch, and spoke with anyone who would listen. It would be misleading to say her intellectual disability was gone, but it was overcome to the point she could enjoy life and the people who surrounded her. She began taking part in group activities. As far as we were all concerned it was a miracle!

## CHEERING FOR ADDISON

As part of the girls' social lives, we do Sports Fridays. It gets very competitive, shockingly competitive. The sports range from swimming to soccer to badminton to volleyball.

## Chapter 5: Lessons in Love

Addison now felt she was ready for her first Sports Friday. I was not so sure, but didn't want to discourage her. What I knew was necessary was to set up the teams so Addison would not be blamed if her team lost.

On this particular Friday, we were playing basketball. The girls were divided into two teams and they had to dribble the length of the court, stopping at the free throw line, and shoot until they made a basket. Once they made their basket, they would bring the ball back to the next girl. The team that could run through their whole line first would be the winner.

I was pretty sure Addison was going to cause her team to lose. Actually, I was confident she was going to take so long to make her basket (if she ever did it) that every girl in the home—including Addison—would know she was the reason her team lost the game. All of us were worried about what this would do to her budding self-confidence. But we wanted to honor the progress she was making by even wanting to play, so we put her on the team we thought would lose for sure. We stacked one team with the best players, and placed Addison as the last player on the other team. Surely the other team would finish before it was Addison's turn, and nobody would care how long it took her to finish.

My strategy was a tremendous fail because when it came to Addison's turn, her team was in the lead! She took the ball, dribbled it to the free throw line, took her shot, and it was nothing but net! For you non-basketball people that means she made the shot her first try. The girls went crazy! Not just the girls on her team, but all of the girls, even those on the losing team, realized they had seen something special. The game ended with every girl in the home chanting "Addison! Addison! Addison!"

## THE POWER OF LOVE

Moments like this in Addison's life were turning points in her care. And that's true for all of the girls in one way or another. It all comes down to love. Here was a girl who had experienced hell on earth to a degree that few on the face of the planet can relate to. And here she was surrounded by a small community that had been proving their love for her day after day. They were celebrating her victories and cheering for her both literally and metaphorically. That's incredibly healing. And in an environment where holistic care is being given, this love takes root and begins to transform the heart. Addison is still affected by her intellectual disability and continues to work through the trauma she's experienced, but she has found substantial healing and is a vital part of our restored community.

Bridget and I, along with our entire team, know full well that we are inadequate for what we are trying to undertake. We have ample proof of how easy it is to fail at this. But because we have experienced the unconditional love of Jesus, we can be conduits of his love. Every one of us who put our faith in Jesus have this opportunity. Because of the transformational power of God's love, "more than we can handle" isn't a problem. God is the one who does the impossible. All he asks us to do is partner with him in loving the people he calls us to serve.

## ARE MIRACLES STILL A PART OF LIFE?

Are miracles still a part of life on earth? In part that may depend upon our definition of a miracle. Some say a miracle defies the laws of nature. I, along with many, would agree. But I believe there are miracles beyond defying the laws of nature: there are the miracles that defy laws of human nature. While I haven't experienced the former, I have the latter, in abundance. Addison is just one of hundreds of examples, including those who were exploiters and abusers of children, later becoming their protectors.

A. W. Tozer says, "God is looking for those with whom he can do the impossible—what a pity that we plan only the things that we can do by ourselves." I agree with Tozer that God is looking for those with whom he can do the impossible; however, I don't believe it is linked to the size of our plans. We may have small plans, but God can do the impossible through them: he can do miracles. The key is stepping out in faith with our small plan through which God can do the impossible. My grandpa and friend Don had the small plan of loving me, and God did a miracle through it. What small plan of yours can God use to make a miracle if you give him the opportunity?

# CHAPTER 6: DAVIDS

## OPENING THE DOOR TO FREEDOM

When Michael Pepe was a captain in the Marine Corps, he was trained to be resilient, tough, intelligent, and resourceful so that he could use those leadership skills to defend his country. But in 2003, when Pepe was fifty years old and retired from the Marines, he moved from California to Cambodia for the purpose of enslaving and abusing very young girls. All of that education and training in leadership and combat would now be put to use destroying several girls well under the age of ten. When federal agents eventually raided Pepe's Cambodian home in June 2006, freeing the enslaved girls and gathering evidence, they said it was the worst case of child abuse they had ever encountered. Take a moment and consider the worst case of child abuse. It's impossible for us to imagine the horror these agents found and what the girls experienced. These children were enslaved by Pepe for months or years, depending on the case. An enslavement where all hope was intentionally and aggressively taken from them.

When Amy and Donna, whom you met in the introduction, were rescued in June 2006, they were just eight and nine years old. Later that year they and three other victims, the oldest eleven years old, were brought to our aftercare home. Michael Pepe was extradited to the US to stand trial for his crimes in Cambodia. At that point the girls began the healing process.

## CAN I GET A WITNESS

In 2007, before the healing process was complete, federal prosecutors came to Cambodia. They asked the girls if they were willing to come to the United

States and testify against Pepe. The prosecutors were patient and kind, and did a great job explaining what it meant to testify. They even set up a room at our home to look like the courtroom where the girls would testify. But I don't think it was possible for these children to truly understand what was to come. Still a decision had to be made. After much prayer and long conversations with each girl it was decided they would testify.

In 2008, these five girls, now ranging in age from nine to twelve years, their counselors and teachers, Bridget, and I boarded a plane headed for Los Angeles, California. The girls were about to enter a world beyond their imaginations.

Once over the jet lag, several weeks of trial prep began. They visited the actual courtroom, a place intimidating to Bridget and me, let alone the girls. The witness box they were to testify from was elevated, which gave each person in the courtroom clear view of them. It was big enough for all five girls to be in it at one time, but they would testify from it one at a time. The seat Pepe was to sit in was just a few feet away and directly in from front them. While it was important for the girls to see the courtroom, the experience did nothing to calm fears—quite the opposite.

Each girl spent hours individually preparing for their testimony. Confidence was waning; one girl decided not to testify. The prosecutors were outstanding in the legal trial prep for the girls, including reviewing the questions they would be asked. Even so there was still the emotional and spiritual impact on these young girls going into a courtroom, with all of its unique and intimidating culture. The weight of bravely facing down the man who had once wielded so much power as he horrifically abused them. Of course their counselors met with them daily, and hundreds of people were praying for them, but Bridget and I felt they needed something more, something tangible to carry into the courtroom to remind them of the truth that they were no longer slaves.

So we told them the story of David from 1 Samuel 17, when David faced the giant Goliath. Goliath was so powerful that the entire Israelite army was afraid of him. David, on the other hand, was so small and inexperienced that his own side was laughing at him. But David had confidence that his God was strong, so he grabbed five smooth stones for his sling from the nearby stream and killed the powerful Goliath with a single stone. We told the girls that they were just like David, and they would be walking into that courtroom with just one stone. We explained that the one stone they would use was *the truth*—that would be their weapon against Michael Pepe,

## Chapter 6: Davids

who was much like Goliath to them. Just like David, when they used the truth against the giant, he would be taken down and he would never be able to hurt any more girls. The girls knew that David was the hero in this story because he relied on God, who is always the true hero. We told the girls that if they bravely entered this fight against Goliath, they would be heroes.

Each girl was given a small stone with the word "truth" painted on it. In addition, each girl was given an ID card to remind her of the truth that she was a hero. On the front of the card it gave their name and printed underneath it said, "I am a hero." On the back was Proverbs 14:12, which says, "A truthful witness saves lives."

As each child was called to testify, and walked into the courtroom to face her abuser, she had the stone in one pocket, her ID card in another, and a teddy bear under her arm.

They marched into the courtroom past the crowd, past the jury, and past Michael Pepe. These girls were exceptionally courageous. Through a translator they were asked and answered very painful questions.

The questions were so horrific and graphic I cannot repeat them here with out making this book X-rated; however, there is one example I'll share. The defense put up a photo of a man's genitals, and asked a girl if she could identify them as Pepe's. She lowered her head in embarrassment and shook her head to say no.

Tears of anger, frustration, and sorrow rolled down my cheeks. I wanted to physically beat the defense attorney and rescue the girl, but I could not do neither. Bridget stayed with and comforted the girls after they testified. I stayed in the courtroom. During a break I asked the prosecutor if the fact that the girl didn't identify the photo as Pepe's genitals would hurt the case. She surprised me by saying, "It helped the prosecution's, our case. Those were not Pepe's genitals, they were trying to trick her."

Can you believe that?! It's legal to lie to a nine year old with a photo like that, in order to defend the accused. That was just the tip of the iceberg of the disturbing things we learned about our justice system. That's stuff for another book.

Testifying was grueling on each girl. Each one shed tears as they were forced to relive the abuse they had suffered. But each little girl, in a foreign courtroom, sitting fifteen feet away from her abuser who was staring at her the whole time, bravely gave her testimony. The judge would kindly ask the girls if they needed a break; the answer was always, "No." Each was determined to tell the truth. Each of the girls sat there in turn like David, each throwing her one small, smooth stone. And Goliath tumbled. The jury deliberated just a few hours. "Monstrous does not begin to capture the horror of the crime or the impact on the victims," US District Judge Dale Fischer said as she sentenced Pepe to 220 years in federal prison.

## ROYAL TREATMENT

During this process, we were in the US for six weeks. As noted earlier we brought counselors and teachers with us so the girls could continue their restoration process and education while we were away from the home in Cambodia. The girls all slept immediately after delivering their testimony, then we would take them to do something fun together.

There were a lot of people who wanted to help the girls in any way they could. They were given a shopping spree at an upscale Salvation Army store. The store was open just for them and they could take all they wanted, for free! We watched with huge smiles as the girls started filling their bag, but when the bag turned into bags, I felt they might be getting a little greedy. I decided to give them a little lesson on greed. As I began the speaking I soon learned they were grabbing things for their sisters back in Cambodia. Sometimes I'm such a schmuck! They selected gifts for every girl in the aftercare home. We had to buy luggage to bring it all back. If we open our hearts and minds, we then realize that we, as teachers, often become students.

The prosecution had set the girls up with an armed guard around the clock, so we had agents escorting us on all of our outings. They fell in love with the girls, it was so clear to everyone. One memorable day we were able to take the girls out on a bike ride. It was so fun to see them simply being kids and riding their bikes along a nearby biking path. Of course, the girls had never ridden on a bike path before, so they were alternating between lanes. At one point one of the girls got in the way of a serious bicyclist trying to cruise down the path. The guy got really angry with this little Cambodian girl, yelling and venting his frustration at being slowed down on his bike ride. One of the agents on the girls' security team stepped up to the angry cyclist and told him to move along. When the guy turned from yelling at the girl to address the plainclothes agent, he yelled in his face, "F— you!" The agent pulled his jacket back to show the guy his gun and badge and calmly replied, "No, f— you." The guy got moving with no further comment. I have to admit, it was satisfying to see people standing

## Chapter 6: Davids

up for these girls who were only beginning to experience a world in which powerful people came to their defense instead of pursuing their destruction. The federal agent apologized for using that word. I told him there was no need for him to apologize.

During this six-week period, we also got to take the girls to the San Diego Zoo for free because one of our staff members had a connection there. The zoo closed down an entire amphitheater and did a private show just for our girls. Each of the children were given the choice to get kisses from a sea lion. When it was Donna's turn, she said she wanted to do it, but every time the sea lion tried to kiss her, she would chicken out and duck down. We tried it three times and finally gave up. I can't tell you how great it felt to see these girls being treated like they're special, like they matter. Because they are and they do. We knew it, and experiences like this helped them believe it.

Before returning to Cambodia we visited Disneyland. They liked everything there, but fell in love with actors dressed as different Disney princesses. I think it was because they believed they were actual princesses. They were told each could pick out just one thing as a souvenir. Each one chose a different princess dress. The girls wore those princess dresses all day, including the uncomfortable plastic shoes that came with the dresses. That day they were dressed like the princesses we told them they were during their orientation to our after care home. They were the heroes their ID cards said they were.

### THE GOOD LIFE

After returning to Cambodia the girls continued through the healing process, and were becoming loving and caring adolescents. Hopelessness was gone, replaced with dreams of a good life. They were unaware those dreams were about to greatly expand. Because they testified in the United States against Michael Pepe they were offered visas that would allow them to move to the States and stay, eventually becoming United States citizens. Each girl jumped at the opportunity.

As you can imagine there were many details involved in making the move to America. The three biggest needs were legal, educational, and a loving home.

Legal was the easiest. Government officials and pro bono immigration lawyers paved the way.

Education was much harder. We needed a pathway for the girls, who knew little English, to enter public high school. We decided to set up a small classroom in our cramped US office and hire a full-time teacher to prepare them for public school. This was no easy task as the girls were clearly on five different educational levels, and needed a lot of loving encouragement. God provided the perfect teacher, Miss Alyssa. A lovely Christian young woman with a heart for those struggling. She was far more than a teacher. She was also a mentor, a friend, and a godly example. In about eighteen months she had the girls ready to move forward with school.

The local high school couldn't have been better, as it provided the extra help needed by students learning English as a second language. The girls continued to be encouraged and loved by their teachers, two of them being AIM supporters. The end result was that all the girls earned a high school diploma. Miss Alyssa and several other teachers continue to be part of the girls' lives.

The most important need was a loving family. A forever family, a place where the girls would be loved unconditionally. Sounds so easy, but it's so incredibly difficult. The first requirement is easy: love Jesus. The rest not so easy. The entire family must be unified in their desire to add a new family member—Mom, Dad, and all the kids. Sharing your life and love with one more family member is not as simple as it sounds. It's easy for jealously to rear its ugly head. Adding a teenage girl to the family, a girl who speaks little English and is suffering from culture shock, will result in painful communication issues.

It was a painstaking process, but eventually God provided five incredibly loving families who he used to guide the girls to the lives they had dreamed about. (If you're one of those families reading this book, you should write a book about your experience.)

Today the girls live in California, Arizona, Texas, and Cambodia. One of the girls serves as a full-time volunteer with AIM in Cambodia. Three others have returned to Cambodia to serve with AIM on a short-term basis. All have shared their experience to help other girls rescued from slavery. Three are married, two have had their own kids. God has transformed them through the people he has placed in their lives, and is using them to bring transformation to others.

## Chapter 6: Davids

**THE GOOD LIFE INTERRUPTED**

Michael Pepe was convicted under the PROTECT Act, a law approved by Congress in 2003. It criminalized the behavior of any US citizen "who **travels** in foreign commerce, and engages in any illicit sexual conduct with another person." In 2013, Congress, in what seemed to be a simple clarification, amended the PROTECT Act to specify that the law applies to a US citizen who travels in foreign commerce or resides, either temporarily or permanently, in a foreign country, and engages in the prohibited sexual conduct.

Based on this amendment Pepe contended that the amendment demonstrated that during 2005 and 2006—the timeframe covering Pepe's offenses—his conduct was not covered by the version of the law in existence. (While Pepe occasionally traveled to the United States during the years he spent in Cambodia, including a trip just three months prior to the timeframe in which the charged conduct occurred, he maintained that he was a formal resident of Cambodia, and therefore outside the scope of the earlier statute. The original law applied only to people traveling to a foreign country, not those who resided in a foreign country.) Based on his appeal and the single word, "travel," the Ninth Circuit Court of Appeals agreed. In July 2018, the court held that the 2013 amendment to the PROTECT Act invalidated Pepe's conviction, finding that the language addition demonstrated the previous version of the law was not intended to cover those who reside in a foreign country. The fact that Pepe had enslaved and sexually abused the girls was never in question: the only issue was whether he traveled to or resided in Cambodia. Because the original jury did not consider this question Pepe was granted a new trial. Delayed by COVID, the new trial was to begin in August 2021.

The federal prosecutor from the first trial was scheduled to prosecute the new trial, but during the delay she was appointed to a federal judgeship. The new team of prosecutors reached out to the five girls and asked if they would once again testify against Pepe. Even knowing what they were about to face, each one said, "Yes!" They didn't want him to hurt another girl.

Again the prosecutors spent a couple of weeks preparing the girls. Unlike the last time, this meant being away from husband, children, other family, and responsibilities back home. When it was time for the trial, it wasn't counselors and teachers who came with them, it was husbands, other family members, loved ones, Bridget, and me.

They were required to share the details of their abuse even though their being abused was not the issue. This was magnified by the fact that Pepe's defense did not cross-examine the girls about their abuse, and even stated in their closing argument that Pepe had abused the girls, but that wasn't the issue.

I believe reliving the abuse they suffered was more difficult, more hurtful than the first trial. At the first trial, being naive in the ways of the world, and speaking through a translator was far from easy, but it was easier than fully understanding what had happened to them and speaking directly to the entire courtroom. Once again, the girls were so courageous in sharing their stories, all five of them this time! I believe Pepe's defense team's claim that abuse wasn't the issue fell on deaf ears. The girls' courageous testimonies were what the jury clearly heard. Michael was found guilty on all counts and again sentenced to 220 years in prison.

After the trial was completed the lead prosecutor from the first case, now a federal judge, invited the girls, Bridget, and me out to dinner. It was a great restaurant, in a beautiful setting. It was an evening with a couple of surprises. The first came as the server approached our table and asked if anyone would like a drink. The girls simultaneously said, "A spicy margarita, please." Now it shouldn't be surprising that twentysomething girls order spicy margaritas, but there is a part of me who will always see these girls as they were the first day that came to our aftercare home.

The second surprise was the real one. After a lovely dinner filled with laughter and love the federal judge said she had something for the girls. She gave each girl her personal cell phone number and her home address. She then said, "If you're ever in the LA area again, please give me a call and stay at my home."

What?! How does that happen? How does the worst of the abused become so transformed that they can impact a judge so deeply she gives them such personal information? It doesn't happen in a few months or even a few years. It takes a lifetime of experiencing the transformational love of Jesus. It takes the staff of aftercare homes, a family opening their hearts and home, and friends who become permanent conduits of Jesus' love.

The girls, Bridget, and I headed back to the hotel where we were staying. Later, we sat by the swimming pool talking. Just as I thought this day couldn't get any better one of the girls spoke up and said, "We must pray for Michael Pepe's salvation." After all he had done to them, they forgave him. I should add they didn't want him to leave prison. God could use him there.

## Chapter 6: Davids

**OPENING OUR HEARTS AND HOMES**

There's a statistic I find alarming in what it says, and how few people know it. Here you go . . .

More than 50 percent of the rescued child victims of sex trafficking in the United States come from the foster care system. In some areas it's as high as 80 percent.

The statistic tells us there is a desperate need for people who passionately love Jesus to get involved in the system. Doing so provides the greatest opportunity to prevent child sex trafficking in the US, and does far more good in the life of an unwanted child. In 2022, *Roe v. Wade* was overturned and there was great celebration among many Christians. I believe this celebration was premature. While I am 100 percent behind fewer abortions, we must recognize fewer abortions means more unwanted kids. Until we Christians determine to take on our responsibility to care for unwanted children, we should pause our celebration.

The greatest need is for foster families, and the responsibility of being a foster family is definitely more than some families can take on. However, there are still many ways for us to get involved by volunteering, some requiring just a few hours a week or less to support a child and/or a foster family. For more information on getting involved please email me at donb@aimfree.org.

# CHAPTER 7: OPEN TO THE UNEXPECTED, BOTH GOOD AND BAD

**GRAB HER AND GO**

You met Carol in the introduction. To jog your memory: Carol's mother sold her when she was twelve to a Chinese man. A trafficker normally gets $8,000 to $10,000 for a virgin, the mother receiving less than 10 percent of it. This man believed he needed to have sex with a virgin so he could gain good luck for his weekend of gambling at the casino. When this same man returned for another gambling trip, Carol's mother, knowing her "soiled" daughter had lost her value, agreed to sell her again. This time the trafficker would receive somewhere around $500. Her mother might have pocketed $50 for this second sale. After that, her mother casually sold her to a brothel a couple of hours away from home.

Somehow, Carol had learned of AIM and found a way to call us and beg us to come and get her. Being entirely noble in my intentions, but completely naive about all of the dynamics involved, I told her, "We'll be there in two days." Why wait two days? In the past when we got a call like this we would do a "grab and go" rescue. We'd tell the brothel owner we wanted to buy the girl, and negotiate a price. Before paying, we would ask them to bring the girl out so we could confirm she was the one we wanted. When she was brought out we'd grab her and go, without paying! This was great for that one girl, but another girl would take her place, then another, then another. The brothel would remain open.

This time we were going to do it the right way. Not only would Carol be rescued, but all the other enslaved girls would be as well. And the brothel would be shut down. So I shared the information Carol gave us about her

## Chapter 7: Open to the Unexpected, Both Good And Bad

circumstances with the police and an NGO. An NGO is a nonprofit organization that typically addresses a social or political issue. In this case the NGO specialized in rescuing the victims of child sex trafficking, working alongside Cambodia's anti-trafficking police. If they were not able rescue Carol with a proper raid in two days, we would go back to our less than perfect method of rescue.

Their investigators confirmed the intel they received and the raid was set for the next day. Tragically, someone tipped off the owner of the brothel and he moved his operation to an undisclosed location. Now we were unable to execute our plan B to rescue Carol.

The brothel owner burst into the room in which he had locked Carol and the other girls. Believing she was the one who got the police involved, he looked into Carol's eyes with arrogance and malice and said, "I own you! I own the police! You're never leaving this place!" There is no natural explanation for what happened next.

I had an unwarranted confidence that we could rescue Carol from her enslavement. She shared my unwarranted confidence and looked at this man, who made his living off of enslaving young girls, and told him defiantly, "I'm not worried about that. AIM is coming to get me." He simply replied, "Well, if they're coming, then you can go." Then he put her on a bus and sent her to us.

Due to God's miraculous intervention, Carol spent a "mere" twenty-two days in sex slavery. During that time, Carol was raped a total of 198 times. Our discovery of the damage inflicted on little girls like Carol over a three-week span increased our urgency to rescue girls exponentially. But we couldn't have imagined the difficulty of getting these girls out.

## LEAKS

The failed raid in Carol's case was just one example of a growing problem we continue to run into. By utilizing people in the local church and pursuing any relationships that could lead to more information, we had developed a strong network of informants. The intel we were gathering from these Cambodian Christians proved so reliable that all of the anti-trafficking organizations around wanted the intel we were getting.

Unfortunately, one scenario continued to unfold: we would find out about girls being trafficked in a specific spot, we would give our intel to one of these groups that conducted raids, they would plan a raid and get ready to execute, and then the bad guys would get tipped off. This is exactly what had happened in Carol's case, but it was about to get worse. In the months ahead, it happened every time we provided intel to a rescuing NGO and the Cambodian police.

No girls rescued, no bad guys arrested in twelve consecutive raids in which we provided the intel. It's hard to describe how demoralizing it can be. It borders on hopelessness. And it's a testament to the power of evil.

Initially, we suspected the Cambodian police were the source of the leak. But then the director of the anti-trafficking group we had been working with sat down with our team and told us they had found the leak. Their investigative team was on the payroll of local traffickers! When the NGO hired a new staff member, the traffickers had casually called him to get him on the payroll, not realizing he wasn't corruptible like all of the others. He had the integrity to tell the national director and the investigating team was dissolved. It was great that the corruption was ended, but now there were even fewer people focusing on rescuing the enslaved girls. It seemed like another step towards hopelessness, but God would show us differently.

## WHAT'S THE YOUNGEST?

On what was a typical day in Svay Pak, Cambodia, a white man in his thirties drove along the main street, a dirt road, and stopped his moped next to a young woman.

She asked, "How can I help you?"

The man looked her in the eyes and said, "Where could I find sex with young girls?"

"Girls? How old do you want?"

The man considered for a minute and then responded, "Young."

The young woman didn't want his answer to be vague. "How old?"

"What's the youngest?"

She needed him to say it himself. "I don't know. How old do you want?"

"Eight, nine, ten, eleven?"

This isn't fiction. That conversation took place in March 2014 when Danny Davila, an American pedophile, unknowingly asked a member of our AIM team—at the time a worship leader at the church in Svay Pak—where he could purchase sex with young girls.

## Chapter 7: Open to the Unexpected, Both Good and Bad

When we first started this ministry, we would yell in the faces of the Western pedophiles who came for what's disgustingly known as "sex tourism." We'd chase them off, but even then we knew it wouldn't do any good. They'd just go to the next location. Now, we have trained some of our team, like this young woman, to wear spy glasses to catch pedophiles in the act of trying to purchase sex with a minor.

Davila's case was not uncommon. These men will ask for young girls, but it's important that they define that term themselves. Our team has to be careful to avoid entrapment, so they lead the men by asking specifically what they want. Sometimes they specify that they want a virgin. When it comes to age, the first number they throw out varies: fourteen, fifteen, ten. Often younger.

In this case, we turned in our undercover footage over to the FBI, who issued a warrant for Davila's arrest. He never stood trial because he pled guilty. He's now behind bars in an American prison.

We have learned again and again that evil is deeply rooted and far reaching. Even after we're able to liberate girls from their captors, they're not entirely free. Often, the girls have been told that if they testify, their families will be harmed. In the Cambodian system, it's rare for girls to be rescued before they get hurt. And the hurt goes far deeper than the physical abuse. Fear lingers longer than chains. Shame follows them everywhere. For these and other reasons, it can be difficult to get girls to testify against their abusers and enslavers, even if those people can be apprehended by the police.

But as we've seen in so many other respects, God's power breaks in. When Carol testified against the people who harmed her, other girls saw her courage and were inspired. When they saw that her abusers were brought to justice and their victims set free, we had other girls coming to us to tell their stories. This wave of bravery allowed us to gather better intel on what was going on in the area. But who would we give this intel to? How could more girls be set free and more bad guys put in jail?

### EVEN THE IMPOSSIBLE

One thing I know for sure: God can do anything. Even the impossible. I've seen this over and over again in the work we've pursued. When you first learn about the evils of trafficking, it's a suffocating experience. Everything in you wants to look away. Most people do, because the problem is too big. There are evil people hiding in the shadows, preying on these young girls. There are powerful people making huge amounts of money by exploiting human beings. There are corrupt governments and police officers. Even the organizations formed to stop this evil are susceptible to infiltration. Even the people who have enough compassion to care about the girls being harmed are unwittingly feeding the system through their use of pornography. Even if you could get a few girls out of the system, how could you make anything any better for them? How could any of us do the slightest thing against the global networks and powerful systems that keep this hell profitable?

It seems obvious that this battle against child sex trafficking is hopeless. Yet, we've seen a dramatic reduction in the amount of trafficking taking place in Svay Pak, Cambodia. A place that was once the epicenter of child sex trafficking in Southeast Asia is now a place where children are loved and protected. It should be impossible, but God is doing it. He is doing it through his people united in love, refusing to look away, and doing their small part with what God has given them.

## A NEW START

Here's more to Carol's story.

This realization of her self-worth has led Carol to take more steps of faith. She decided that she wanted to be a social worker so she could help to rescue and restore girls who were experiencing the pain she knew so well.

While she worked in the bracelet room, Carol's boss was a young man named Doug. He had grown up in a Cambodian orphanage that was shut down when it was discovered that children were being abused. He was eventually able to go to a Christian college in New York, and when he graduated and returned to Cambodia, we hired him to manage our bracelet production. He was and is an awesome Christian man. They were interested in each other, but didn't want to pursue it because of their work relationship. But once she became a social worker with our SWAT team (more on the SWAT team in the next chapter), there was no longer an obstacle to the possibility of a relationship.

Doug is a respectable young man, so he asked Bridget and I if he could take Carol on a date. I loved finding myself in this situation. We told him that he couldn't go on a date, but if he wanted to spend time with her in a group setting, that would be fine. Doug said yes to any stipulations we put

CHAPTER 7: OPEN TO THE UNEXPECTED, BOTH GOOD AND BAD

on the way he began interacting with Carol. I was enjoying the powerful position I was in here, but we eventually told him he could take her on a date. We had to laugh when he showed up to pick her up for their first one-on-one date and found that Carol had invited her siblings to join them!

Eventually, Doug asked our permission to marry Carol. We enthusiastically told him yes and he quickly proposed. We experienced the unbelievable beauty of redemption as we attended Carol's engagement party. A while later I officiated her wedding. Tears of joy come easily for me at the wedding of a loved one. They overflowed at this wedding!

## MEANWHILE IN CHINA

When we first got involved in Cambodia, it was because God put the dilemma of these young Cambodian girls in our path, and we couldn't look away. We had thrown ourselves into this fight through making a series of small decisions that continued to expand the ministry.

One day, one of our social workers got a call from a panicked Cambodian girl in China. She said, "Please help me. I was forced to marry a man who bought me. I've run away, but I need someone to get me before they find me!" This was out of the blue. We had more than enough to do in Cambodia. But this young woman had called a friend asking for help, and her friend told her, "Here's the number for AIM; call them and they'll rescue you."

Once again we felt the Lord was placing a critical situation in front of us and asking us not to look away.

Here's how this works. There is a whole trafficking industry that sells brides to Chinese men. A few of these girls know they are going to China to be married, but most often traffickers go into garment factories and target young women. They tell them, "You can make a lot more money doing the same thing in China. We can take care of the whole process for you. We'll get you the passport and arrange your transportation." All of this sounds appealing to someone who works long hours for little money. It looks like a dream come true, the end to hopelessness.

So these girls agree to the arrangement, then once they arrive in a Chinese village, far from their homes and without any idea of how to get home, their passports are taken away from them and they are held captive. After a while, they are lined up while men come in to choose a bride. Most of these men are poor men who have taken out a loan for the roughly $12,000

US required to purchase a bride. Once the girls are chosen, the women are moved to a town where they don't know the language, they don't really know their location, and they are forced to function as household slaves and to provide an heir for their "husbands." Many are beaten, raped, and abused. Once the men get the heir they wanted, they can resell the girl to repay the loan they had taken out to purchase her in the first place.

This story is exceedingly common in China because there are so many more men than women in that country. The Chinese government had made and enacted the one-child policy. The misogynistic nature of the culture led most couples to choose a male child and many female children were aborted. With this major shortage of women, trafficking brides is big money. (In May 2021 the Chinese amended the law to allow a couple to have up to three children. While it is encouraging to see the change it will be years before it impacts the ratio between men and women of marrying age.)

This is a major problem, but we had no intention of getting involved. And then we received that phone call. It turns out that the friend this young woman who called had been trafficked to China herself. This is where they had met. But the friend had somehow escaped with two other girls and miraculously found the right people to take them back to Cambodia. Once they arrived in Cambodia, we were asked to help care for them and get them reintegrated into their communities. We did what was needed for them, but we didn't expected it to pull us into the world of bride trafficking in China.

Once we received that phone call, we could choose to look away. Or we could say yes to this one person and do what we could.

So we talked to the Cambodian general of cross-border trafficking and told him what was happening. He agreed to work with us. The first step was to have this girl flee to the Cambodian embassy in Beijing. But when we communicated this to her, she told us that she had already gone to the embassy asking for help and they had told her to go back. The general spoke to her directly and told her, "Don't worry. This time will be different. I'll have everything set up. Go back to the embassy again."

Not long after, we got another phone call from this girl. She had brought a friend who also wanted to escape, and they had gone to the embassy together. But once again, they were being told to go back. We told her, "Don't worry, we'll get hold of the general. Don't let them send you back."

In order to just reach the embassy, these poor girls had been running and hiding. They hadn't had anything to eat or drink for five days. The

## Chapter 7: Open to the Unexpected, Both Good and Bad

friend decided she couldn't go on any longer, so she gave herself up and went back to her horrible situation. The girl who had called us was stronger and decided to wait and hope. Honestly, I didn't know at the time if her hope would be rewarded.

We couldn't get anyone at the embassy to help, so I started thinking of people I knew who might be able to help. All of this was a long shot, but we had a strong supporter from Hong Kong named Lisa who had a business in Beijing. I called her and explained the situation. It turns out she was in Beijing at that very moment. I asked her to go to the embassy and pick up this girl herself—is that a reasonable request?—and she simply said, "Okay, I'll go."

She felt her husband might not want her to go, so Lisa quietly left the hotel they were staying at without telling him. She then asked her driver to take her to the Cambodian embassy.

Lisa called a little later and said the Cambodian girl wouldn't leave with her. Seems she didn't trust someone who appeared to be an official. We called the girl and told her she could trust Lisa, and to please go with her. Problem solved.

Well, not yet solved. Lisa called us and told us that the embassy security guards were not letting them leave. I told her, "Lisa, you're going to have to man up. You grab that girl by the arm and take her to the car and just drive away!"

Lisa was obviously nervous. She said, "Really?"

"Yes. You just have to do it."

After we waited for a few minutes that felt like a really long time, we finally got a call back from Lisa:

"I've got her! I've got her!" she said. "Now what do I do with her?"

Our plan hadn't developed that far, so I started thinking again of who else I knew that could help. We had another supporter who managed a beautiful hotel in Beijing. He didn't know it, but he was about to become an abolitionist as well. (Is this making you want to become a supporter of AIM?)

I called him and explained the situation. I told him that we needed a safe place for this girl to stay until we could work out the details of bringing her home. I suggested she might be able to stay in their staff housing. To my relief, he said yes. But instead of the staff housing he put her on the executive level of his hotel! This sweet girl went from nearly starving as she literally ran away from slavery to getting room service three times a day in a luxury hotel.

Bridget and I immediately flew to Beijing to figure out how to get her home to Cambodia. While I worked with the embassy and the police, Bridget took her shopping and bought her a few things. We were able to get things moving for her return, while we returned to Cambodia.

By the time everything came together and this girl was able to come back home, she had lived on the top floor of a five-star hotel for two months! Of course, none of this erased the pain she had experienced. And sadly, she had to leave her baby behind when she fled. We were able to give her a small loan so she could start a business and get reestablished. Lisa was able to come visit her later in Cambodia and experience the joy of seeing the miraculous fruit that comes with being available when God calls.

Once again, we weren't trying to start a ministry to help trafficked brides in China, but now we couldn't look away. We learned that in order to work with the anti-trafficking police in China, we had to get a case file started for each of the girls that would eventually ask us for help.

It's rare for these young women to have access to a phone with the money to call us and share enough information to build a case file. We created a toll-free hotline to remove that obstacle. Now, girls could call us for free and give us the information we needed to work with the police and help them escape. We've never advertised that hotline; it passes only through word of mouth.

In the first five years the hotline was active, we helped dozens of Cambodian girls return from China. Since then things have slowed, we hope in some part to a video. We created a video of one of the rescued girls sharing her story that our social workers show to the vulnerable garment factory workers and others living around the factories. The goal is to help girls understand the dangers in being offered a job that seems "too good to be true" and avoid being trafficked.

## ONE MORE THING

Initially, I was going to skip this story and go right to the conclusion of the chapter. After all, this book will not be long enough for all the stories. But this story is a little different as to how someone's tiny step of faith can lead many others to their small or even big steps of faith.

## CHAPTER 7: OPEN TO THE UNEXPECTED, BOTH GOOD AND BAD

Our aftercare home was finally firing on all cylinders. We had a great staff and God was using them to bring healing to dozens of girls. It was then our email brought some disturbing news. A large donation that would be arriving to finance our next quarter of expenses would be delayed three months. The good news was it would come, the bad news was we wouldn't have the funding to pay our staff for three months! We knew this would result in many members of our staff, who made up the well oiled machine of our aftercare, having to leave to work elsewhere. Before making a plan to muddle through the next three months we met with the staff to apprise them of the situation.

We gave them the news, letting them know we understood some, maybe many, would need to look for a new job. Their response shocked us!

They said, "Don't you know we love the girls as much as you do? This is our ministry too! We will stay and trust God to provide for us until the funding comes!"

Not a single team member resigned.

I'm surprised that while typing this story years later my eyes still well with tears.

### START WITH THE NEED YOU SEE

As I keep repeating, this didn't start with a strategy to attack the problem of bride trafficking. It started with saying "yes" to that one person who was standing before us. We could choose to say yes or no to this one person. Choosing not to look away has opened up countless doors for continual healing for so many people. When we take small steps of faith like this, it's incredible to see what God will do, how he will provide all we need. Even the needs we don't realize.

If we had known everything that God would eventually lead us to do, we probably would have been too intimidated to have started at all. But truly we only took one step of faith at a time. As we saw God meet impossible needs time after time, we began to understand how he was working. We began to expect him to do what we couldn't do through our small steps of faith. And we expected he would provide for us to overcome all the obstacles we never anticipated.

The question: what need do you see? Is there a need in your family, church, community... in the world, that God is asking you to take a small step of faith to meet? It may be as small as helping someone you know in need of encouragement, or as big as standing with the oppressed and fighting injustice. Our experience is that wherever you start God will take you further than you expect.

# CHAPTER 8: SWAT

## FINDING A NEXT STEP

GOD WAS GRACIOUS IN allowing us to recover Carol. He literally led her straight to our door. But as you can imagine, we were rattled by the leaks that shut down so many raids. God can help these girls however he wants to, and he had proven that he didn't need our help at all to pull a girl out of her captivity. But we also knew that he had led us to Cambodia to do something to help these children, and we were not okay with the idea that raids were simply impossible because leaks were inevitable. We knew there had to be another way forward.

I won't surprise you by saying that as a former pastor, I had no experience with SWAT teams or raids or toppling trafficking organizations. All I knew is that girls were in serious danger and God wanted to do something about it. A few years into our work in Cambodia, I had enough experience with saying "yes" to the things God was putting in our path to know that if God was presenting us with a problem, he would give us a way forward, an opportunity to move forward in faith. In this case he was working far upstream.

A couple of years prior to our knowing anything about Carol, CNN aired a documentary called *Not My Life*, which exposed the extent of human trafficking around the world. In making the film they stopped in Cambodia and conducted a short interview with me. CNN aired the film across the globe, including Cambodia. Immediately after the film aired they selected a few people to interview live on air. I was one of them.

At the time I was frustrated by what I believed was lack of effort on the part of the Cambodian government to stop child sex trafficking. I figured no one in Cambodia would be watching CNN, so I didn't hold back in the interview. I complained about the situation as a whole and about the police in particular. Although I knew there wouldn't be any actionable results, it was cathartic.

Imagine my surprise the next morning when there was a government car waiting outside my house. Officials came to my door and told me that the general over anti-trafficking police in Cambodia wanted to have a chat. It turned out that at least some Cambodian generals watched CNN, and had the opportunity to hear all of my comments about how the government was failing in this area. As soon as I sat down in his office, he let me have it. He didn't appreciate having a foreigner come into his country and start complaining to the world about how bad the government was.

By this point, I had seen too many of the horrors these girls were experiencing to care about this general's PR concerns, or what he may have decided to do with me. So I openly shared all my concerns and what evidence I had to support them.

I was shocked at his response. His purpose was not so much to silence me, but to hear from me. He cared greatly for the child victims of sex trafficking and wanted to rescue them, and put away the bad guys. I explained we were beginning to get solid intel from our church members in Svay Pak and we wanted it to be used in the most effective manner. He asked me to give it to a specific NGO who his team worked with to fight sex trafficking. My enthusiastic answer was, "You can count on us!"

While this NGO was not the one with the corrupt investigative team in the previous chapter, they were no more successful than them. What were we to do now?

## LAUGHED OUT OF THE ROOM

I had read that when the US military was operating in Afghanistan, they would work in conjunction with the local Afghanis. A simple thought came to me in the shower one day: "Why don't we create our own SWAT team that works and trains with the local police and has the power to arrest people?" I recognize that a sane person might dismiss a thought like that, but Bridget and I felt there was something to it, so I put together a proposal for a SWAT team.

I first went to another anti-trafficking organization and ran the idea by them. They were nice enough to tell me the idea sounded good, but they told me with certainty that I would get laughed out of the room if I

## Chapter 8: SWAT

tried presenting an idea like that to the government. I talked to another anti-trafficking group and they said exactly the same thing. Everyone with any experience in this area was telling me it wouldn't work and advised me not to try. Don't waste your time. Don't embarrass yourself. But I couldn't keep looking away.

As I weighed these reactions, I mentally lined up the alternatives. On the one hand, I might be laughed at for an idea. On the other hand, girls were being sold and languished in hopelessness. So I thought, "What the hell? I've been laughed at before. I can handle that if there's a chance it might do something to help these girls."

Because of my "visit" to the general, I knew he was the person I needed to speak with, and convince that the SWAT team was a good idea. In the crazy way that God works, he had during this same period brought me a SWAT team leader. He was a former UK detective named Eric Meldrum who had grown disillusioned with his work in Britain and was involved with anti-trafficking work for another organization in Cambodia. When that organization folded, Eric was eager to work with us, because in his previous role, he had benefited from the intel we were gathering. And unlike everyone else, Eric was enthusiastic about the idea.

When we went to present the proposal to the general, I was fully expecting him to say "no." Nevertheless, I was happy to at least bring this qualified SWAT team leader with me.

The meeting was excruciating. Our proposal was long and the general read every page slowly as we sat there waiting. It was many pages of details ranging from equipment to standard operating procedures. We included many details so we could sell the concept, but now we had to wait while the general slowly read through the proposal page by page.

I just wanted him to get to the end. I knew he would say "no." And we were prepared with many counterarguments we hoped would change his mind. When he finally got to the last page of the proposal, he set it down on the desk and said, "Let's do it!"

I was shocked! Actually, I was angry. My thought in that moment was, "We've prepared all these counterarguments and now I don't even get to use them!"

With the general's approval, we were now cleared to seek the approval of the head of the Cambodian police. Once again we presented our proposal and waited for the "no" so we could present our counterarguments. Yet again, we received an immediate "yes." It was clearly evident that God was moving. I had mustered up my courage to endure being laughed at and it turns out I didn't hear a single snicker. Every informed person had told us not to try, but God had plans. It didn't matter what anyone else considered impossible. It didn't matter that it seemed like a long shot. We had said "yes" to God's call and he opened the path forward.

One small obstacle remained, however, before we could launch our SWAT team. We needed $250,000 to get things going! I was pretty confident we were the only Christian ministry with a government-approved SWAT team, which is pretty cool. However, it also provided a unique challenge: finding a church who would fund it.

Here again God was moving. Ray Johnston, the pastor of Bayside Church in Northern California, had just reached out to me. The church was doing their annual Christmas offering and he wanted to know if we had anything going on that could use some extra funding. When I told him what we were trying to do, his question was, "Do you need weapons and bulletproof vests and all that kind of stuff?"

I told him we needed all of it. He was hesitant at first. What pastor wouldn't be? After some prayerful consideration with his staff, he responded, "We'll do it!" I don't remember the official name for the church's Christmas offering, but I heard it referred to as "Bullets for Jesus."

Against all odds, we suddenly had a SWAT team.

## INFORMANTS AND INVESTIGATORS

We knew that one of the most important aspects of having our own SWAT team would be gathering our own intelligence. We had actually been building an intelligence network through the local church since we started AIM. When Eric Meldrum agreed to lead our SWAT team, he told us one of the main reasons he wanted to join us was that we were the only ones in the area getting consistently reliable intel. It wasn't one or two bits of information, our informants were specific and they were regularly giving us reliable intel. That gave us a solid start, and Eric and his team worked to expand our network of informants.

Sometimes our investigators work undercover, other times they do simple surveillance. When we first started AIM, it wasn't difficult to gather this information. Many of the brothels in Cambodia looked like street-level massage parlors, but it's not hard to figure out that any place offering massages for $2 wouldn't be able to stay in business. Places like that were easy to spot. Other places would set themselves up as coffee shops. They would actually sell coffee, so our team could go in there and buy coffee. It wasn't long, however, before the young girls would start talking to them and the woman in charge would bluntly offer to sell the girls.

Also, many Cambodian karaoke bars, called "KTVs," will sell girls in addition to running a karaoke establishment. If the customers were trusted and knew who and how to ask, they could purchase girls to take with them to fulfill their depraved fantasies. As the traffickers have grown more subtle, we've had to adjust to gain their trust over time. They have learned to move the girls around and make it difficult to know who will be where and when. Sometimes they'll even ask us outright if we are police. Because we've been able to make a dent in the trafficking, the traffickers have had to make changes, become more covert in their operations. This is especially true with the very young girls who provide the greatest profit. Evil has historically evolved, and it continues to do so.

We have to carefully decide who we can send in to earn the trust of the people running each establishment. If the place is "higher class," we'll be sure to send our investigators in with plenty of money and with all the props that make them look like high rollers. We work hard to make sure we're perceived as normal customers. It is heart-wrenching to go in and not immediately help, but in conjunction with the Cambodian anti-trafficking police we've rescued a lot of girls this way. We have to be careful that the right people are being arrested, and be certain enough evidence is gathered to successfully prosecute them. We must avoid "entrapment," where it's clear that you're coaching someone to say the wrong things so they get themselves arrested. Our team is highly trained to earn trust, get information, and then act at the right time.

As time went by investigators found it harder and harder to get the intel we needed to rescue the youngest girls. The brothels were no longer obvious and the managers became far more careful before offering the youngest girls up for their customers. We needed a new kind of investigator.

## INVESTIGATORS 2.0

The best investigator would be someone who knew all the details of a brothel operation. Someone who would not raise the suspicions of brothel operators. In fact, the perfect investigator would be welcomed in and openly shared with. Our first perfect investigator was once a victim of sex slavery;

her name is Sophia. Today Sophia bravely enters the kind of places where she was once enslaved and gathers the intel to set free current victims and arrest their enslavers. Her incredible success has enabled our SWAT team to rescue the youngest victims. It has also led to our adding two more investigators just like her. Sophia shares her story in Appendix 1 of this book.

## RAIDS

We work with Cambodian government prosecutors to ensure that we are collecting all of the evidence we need to actually put the traffickers away. Once we have the prosecutor's approval, we plan a raid in conjunction with the Cambodian anti-trafficking police. We have found that the government and the police want to crack down on trafficking, but there are many factors that make it difficult for them to do it alone. Because the country has been so war-torn and impoverished from the horrifying tyranny and genocide under Pol Pot and the Khmer Rouge, there are many factors stacked against them. Women are often treated very poorly (remember the proverb about boys being gold and girls being cloth?).

Poor families are often offered and accept predatory loans. When they are unable to pay back the lender they believe the only apparent way out is selling a child! But we have found the vast majority of the police do want their country to heal and get better. They do not want Cambodian children enslaved. However, they are hugely under-resourced. They lack the funding and training to do robust investigations. When we team up with the police to do raids, we will pay for key tools like bulletproof vests, batons, and handcuffs to allow them to do their jobs a bit more safely and effectively. Often, we'll even pay for basic things like putting fuel in their cars! In truth, the police have proven that they are willing to take risks and do the right thing, and we have been able to empower them to be more effective.

Once we're ready to execute a raid, our goal is to make sure that all of the victims are rescued, all of the bad guys are arrested, and all of the evidence is collected. Every time, by far, our top priority is rescuing the girls. While the rest of it is important, our raids are victim centered.

It doesn't typically look like it does in the movies, where Liam Neeson is kicking down doors and shooting dead all kinds of bad guys. For example, there usually aren't doors to kick down because these places are typically open to the public. Sometimes we get to kick in a door, but in most cases, we have a scene under control within a few minutes without using

## Chapter 8: SWAT

violence. Still, it's always an adrenaline rush because you can never control the entire situation and you never really know what you'll be faced with. You might encounter security or customers who have guns. Most often, the surrounding community will be happy to see the brothel go, but we never know if there are people in the community who will help the traffickers escape and relocate. Even though we've now done hundreds of raids, it's always a bit chaotic with all of the unknown elements, and we are always nervous for our teams who are bravely entering potentially dangerous and uncontrollable situations to rescue these girls.

Once we've removed the victims and apprehended the traffickers, the place gets officially locked down by the police. We have a team of social workers that will go immediately to the police station with the rescued victims to support and care for them. Within twenty-four hours, the prosecutor will make key decisions about whether or not the rescued girls can be sent to our aftercare home, but the girls will typically spend that first day in the police station giving their testimony. Our social workers sleep at the station with the girls and stay with them every step of the way. The police have allowed us to outfit a room to provide a comfortable overnight stay for the girls. Our legal team helps with the interviews, works with the police, and helps the prosecutors get all of the information they need, right up to the end of the trial.

## CONTINUING TO DO THE IMPOSSIBLE

We have been doing a few raids every month for a long time now, and have rescued more than 2,000 girls and arrested over 500 traffickers. We could always manage more raids with the information we get from our intelligence network and investigators, but we've had to slow ourselves down because we have limited resources with regard to our SWAT team and our aftercare home capacity.

There is rarely a raid in which we don't rescue someone and arrest someone. We do our homework beforehand to ensure that raids are successful. We rarely have tip-offs now. We have seen the few corrupt police get frozen out. We have even had the police in many Cambodian provinces reach out to us before we ask them to work on cases. The entire situation has changed dramatically from when we started.

All of this was considered impossible. When God placed this idea into our hearts, we were told not to tell anyone lest we be ridiculed. Can you imagine if we had kept quiet out of fear of being laughed at? I think of the hundreds of girls we have rescued and I wonder what would have happened to them if we listened to the "experts." Would even one of the girls have been rescued?

Keep in mind all of this was and is outside of my control. I didn't know how to start a SWAT team. But God provided Eric when we needed a SWAT team leader. God provided CNN when we needed light to be shed on the situation. God provided an open-minded general when we needed government support. God provided an informant network when we needed to find brothels to raid. Every piece of it seems utterly impossible. We didn't know how to do any of this! Yet, God put us in the right place at the right time, and taught us to say "yes" when he called us to act. We have so much still to learn, but I pray that we will never forget that saying "yes" to God's impossible call is always the right answer.

So what is God calling you to? What has he put on your heart? Is it fighting trafficking? If so, please reach out! We have so many ways we could use your gifts. Maybe God has put something very different on your heart. Maybe you feel utterly inadequate to do anything about it. Maybe other people have laughed at you for your God-given dreams. Maybe, like Sarah, you've been the one to laugh in God's face when he has placed a dream before you (Gen 18:13).

I don't know what your situation is, but I am here to tell you that I've experienced conclusive proof that God is able to do the impossible. He knows who you are. He knows your strengths and weaknesses. He also knows what he wants to accomplish in this world through you. He wants to use all of us to accomplish bigger things than we can imagine.

The question:

Will we say yes to the One, the opportunity God is giving us to do good? Will we risk being ridiculed for attempting to do the good that seems foolish to the others?

# CHAPTER 9: SVAY PAK

## STATELESS

ALONG THE BANKS OF the Tonle Sap and Mekong Rivers in Cambodia lives what *The New York Times* called the largest group of stateless people in the world—ethnic Vietnamese dwelling in a foreign country. We're not talking about the highest percentage, but the largest population in the world, in one of the smallest countries in the world. How did they get there?

I'll give you the short answer; the full answer is a book in itself. Pol Pot and the Khmer Rouge took over Cambodia in April 1975, but their reign was short. They were defeated by Vietnam in January 1979, and Cambodia became a vassal state. Many of the poorest Vietnamese citizens relocated to Cambodia. However, the extent of damage done by the Khmer Rouge, combined with the United States economic boycott of Cambodia and reduction in aid from the Soviet Union, led Vietnam to withdraw from Cambodia in September 1989. The United Nations stepped into the void.

Many, maybe most, of the poor Vietnamese who relocated to Cambodia stayed. These people are unwanted by both countries. They are struggling to create a life for themselves in a world between two countries: the one they come from that doesn't want them and the one they limped their way into that also doesn't want them. To say that life is difficult for these Cambodian-Vietnamese grossly understates the situation. They can't obtain a government-issued ID, so they are unemployable. They are also unable to own property, so most of them live in floating houses that they've built along the rivers' shorelines. Most of these displaced people feed their families with fish they catch from the river. Some spend their nights combing through other people's trash in search of recyclables to sell for meager fees.

This is a people living on the edge: on the edge of their country of origin, on the edge of their country of refuge, on the edge of survival. As such, these people are highly vulnerable to anyone who has an interest in exploiting destitute people for their own gain. Tragically, there are many such people. As a result, many of these young Vietnamese girls fall prey to child sex traffickers.

Sherry grew up in one of these families. She knew the poverty that pervades a displaced community like this. She knew the hunger that comes from the daily possibility of being unable to acquire enough food to feed the family of six into which she was born. Her floating home was in such desperate need of repair that it was sinking into the river. Her mother faced the unimaginable choice between paying to have her home saved from sinking or feeding her family. In reality, though, "choice" isn't the right word, because there wasn't money for either option. So Sherry's mother did what many of these families do: she took advantage of a small loan from a village loan shark. As you might imagine, these loans are not designed to help the families who take them. Though the loan wasn't for a large enough amount to truly solve their problems, the interest rate was 10 percent per day! Sherry's mom and her entire family were stuck from the moment they accepted the loan. (It's interesting to note that the microloans that raise people out of poverty in many countries aren't available in Cambodia. Cambodian microloans carry interest rates that aren't significantly different from loan sharks'.)

As the interest mounted, they obviously had no means of repaying the rapidly growing debt. As Sherry's mother was unable to pay the debt day after day, the threats from the loan shark grew increasingly violent. Desperate and afraid, her mom agreed to sell the only thing of value available to her: Sherry's virginity.

This scenario is tragically common amongst these displaced Vietnamese throughout Cambodia, and with stateless people in far too many parts of the world. In Sherry's case, after unimaginable suffering caused by the aftermath of her mother's impossible situation and horrifying choice, she found the kind of rescue and restoration that we've been describing throughout this book. Today she is a confident, successful young woman. She is even helping to support the mother who sold her!

As proud as we are of the kind of work that rescues, restores, and reintegrates women like Sherry, we weren't content with helping only after these girls had suffered. So as we learned more about the needs and the

## Chapter 9: Svay Pak

culture and what makes people vulnerable in Cambodia, we began to devote significant efforts toward transforming neighborhoods and working to prevent the conditions that make trafficking easier.

## SVAY PAK

Svay Pak was one of those villages along the Tonlé Sap river, and the place Sherry and her family lived. As you'll remember from a previous chapter, Svay Pak was known around the world as a village where pedophiles and sex tourists were welcomed. On our second trip to Cambodia to learn how we might help, we were physically restrained from entering Svay Pak. But since that time, it was common knowledge that child sex trafficking was no longer happening there. We were about to learn, on its own, never trust common knowledge.

Our social workers were heading out to conduct follow-up visits with the first two girls reintegrated back into Cambodian society after finding healing in our aftercare home. As part of our effort to keep the girls connected to the love of Jesus and to the AIM family they are eternally a part of we followed up with each one on a monthly basis. I decided to tag along and check out that once infamous village.

The village lies eleven kilometers outside of Cambodia's capital city of Phnom Penh. It is split into two parts by the main road leading north toward the city of Siem Reap. On the western shore there are steep banks falling down to the Tonlé Sap river and hundreds of floating homes. "Homes" is probably a poor choice of words. On a good day, they barely kept the weather out, and were always at risk of sinking. On the crest of the bank stood hundreds of tiny shack-like homes so close together the sunshine had a hard time breaking through. All of this was tied together by a network of dirt paths just wide enough for a moped. It smelled of the rotting trash that was strewn everywhere, fish, and a polluted river as wide as the Mississippi.

The other side of the village was significantly larger. A dirt road large enough to handle a car or truck went down the middle. On each side of this road were an array of different sized brick buildings—most, I would learn, were closed brothels. Off the main road were shack-like homes jammed together. And like the other side, all of this was connected by narrow dirt paths. The village was dirty and depressing. An incredibly heavy and dark spirit seemed to fall everywhere.

The social workers headed down to the river while I decided to stroll down the dirt road on the other side of the village. It seemed counterintuitive that such a dark and heavy spirit would be present in a place freed from the evil of child sex trafficking. I was soon to find out the truth.

About halfway down the road a young man came up to me and asked, "Would you like to buy a young girl?"

That was shocking. More shocking was the fact that this pimp was the same one who was in the news special that led to our move to Cambodia. This was the same young man who was supposed to be in prison!

For a moment I thought I was an undercover agent and responded yes to his question. He led me along the narrow pathways to one of the larger shacks, opened the door, and I saw several dozen sets of eyes staring blankly at me. The girls looked to range in age from nine or ten years to the early teens. The pimp said, "Choose who you want and we will go to the place for sex."

It was then I realized I was not an undercover agent. I had no plan and had foolishly put myself in danger. Fear and worry began to cloud my mind. In the end it was truth that set me free. I nervously responded, "I don't have money now, I will come back." Hustling along the dirt path, I found the main road.

Not long after I reconnected with our social workers, anxious to share my experience. Before I could share, they began telling me about their experience. As they spoke, tears filled their eyes. There was no follow-up meeting with the girls, both were missing. Their families and neighbors all insisted they didn't know where the girls were. It's likely they were both once again victims of child sex trafficking.

We had conducted family and community assessments before sending these girls home to assure their safety. But we had naively believed common knowledge and the word of families and neighbors who said they were changed people because of all they had learned from our social workers. That would never happen again!

The truth is only Jesus defeats evil—"only his love can transform hearts" wasn't new to us, but it was indelibly imprinted on our hearts and minds through this experience. It was now up to us to apply this truth. We would start with Svay Pak.

## Chapter 9: Svay Pak

## JESUS VISITS SVAY PAK

We decided the easiest way to build relationships with the community was through the children. We would to start with a kids' club. We would invite all the children in the village to attend a fun time of arts and crafts, singing and dancing, and stories about Jesus. The arts and crafts portion would be taught by girls from our aftercare home, girls who had been healed by Jesus' love and were nearing the time of their reintegration into Cambodian society. It was voluntary. Every eligible girl enthusiastically said "yes" to being a conduit of Jesus' love to the children of Svay Pak. The rest of the club would be led by a children's pastor named Ratanak. But first we needed a place to meet.

We met with the village leader, who was less than warm and fuzzy, and he introduced us to a man with a building to rent, a former brothel. The thought of using what was a place of evil to shine Jesus' love and goodness was exciting. The building, however, was not! Only the front room, about twenty feet by forty feet, was in usable condition. Behind it lay seventeen tiny rooms which in the past were used to hold girls captive while they waited for the next man to come in and rape them. The locks were on the outside of the doors. They now were covered with years of dust, dirt, spiderwebs, and a nauseating musty smell. The rooms were now the home of tarantulas, rats, and snakes. Still, all the space we needed to get started was the front room, so I began negotiating rent.

I met with the owner in a coffee shop in Svay Pak; we sat opposite each other at a tiny table. I asked him how much it would cost to rent the place. He responded, "I like you. I will give the same rent I got five years ago. No increase." He then slid across the rental agreement from five years ago. The rent was $3,000 a month!

I responded, "I was thinking $500 a month."

In anger he pounded his fist on the table and said, "I want $5,000 a year!"

While not a math major, I recognized this as a great deal and happily said, "Yes." We were on the way to making Jesus a regular visitor to Svay Pak!

To advertise our first kids' club the girls volunteering from our aftercare home went around the village with their social workers posting flyers and personally inviting people they encountered. This was a Monday. The kids' club would meet the following Thursday at 2 PM, and every Thursday after that.

The volunteers were so excited about being able to help to other children experience the love of Jesus that it made three days seem like three years. Finally, Thursday arrived. The building was open, everyone and everything in its place, and we all sat waiting in great anticipation. Our anticipation and excitement waned as 2:15 PM rolled around and not a single kid had shown up. The local police had torn down the flyers and went door-to-door telling parents not to send their children. It seemed they were afraid of what might happen if Jesus infiltrated the village.

Undeterred, our girls and social workers went out to the nearby houses and re-invited the children they encountered. About twenty-five children showed up that first day, and the group would grow to between forty and fifty over the weeks to come. In the future it would grow to over three hundred children, meeting five days a week. But we're not to that part of the story yet.

During those initial weeks the children shared with us how some families had little food and were hungry all the time. In response we expanded the ministry to include distributing some rice to the neediest of families and sharing devotions on Sunday mornings.

As the weeks went on we could see that when Jesus visited Svay Pak, through us or other ministries, good things happened to the few people who came out, but not lasting change, not heart transformation. There was no revival. Our goal of preventing child sex trafficking was not happening. It became clear to me that Jesus needed to live in Svay Pak, twenty-four hours a day, 365 days a year.

# CHAPTER 10:
# JESUS MOVES TO SVAY PAK

**THE FIRST STEP**

WE DECIDED JESUS WOULD move to Svay Pak through a church plant, a church with ministries designed to meet what seemed to be the community's greatest needs. This would allow us to build relationships through which God could work. The first task was finding the right pastor, someone with a combination of persevering love, the boldness to confront evil, and the faith to withstand the forces of evil who would attack when confronted. And one more thing: the pastor must be willing to answer God's call to move his or her family to the hellhole of Svay Pak. We began praying.

An Unlikely Candidate

In the course of our aftercare for girls who were rescued from sex trafficking, we met a Cambodian man named Chantha. His first role with us was as a security guard and driver at our aftercare home. Chantha was drawn to our ministry because he was a Christian. Actually, Chantha had studied in a Korean Bible college. For Chantha, however, as with so many who study the Bible through higher education in Cambodia, studying the Bible was a primarily academic exercise. When Chantha came onboard with AIM, we invited him and three other men on staff to do a daily Bible study with me. I called these four our "Mighty Men" and we focused the entire study on nothing but application. We would read some Scripture together and then focus our entire discussion on one question: What are we going to do today because of what we see written here in God's word? Chantha caught on fire from that approach to Scripture, and his life was never the same.

As a boy, Chantha's father had fought for the Cambodian military. This was a particularly dangerous time to serve in the Cambodian military, or to be a Cambodian at all. Pol Pot and his Khmer Rouge were set on a dictatorial overthrow of the Cambodian government and complete control of Cambodian society. Their methods were notoriously cruel and resulted in the murder of a huge percentage of the population and the demoralization and traumatization of the rest of Cambodian society.

Chantha was not unique in having witnessed the Khmer Rouge murder his father. Later, when the Vietnamese came in, Chantha was not unique in having witnessed his mother gang raped by Vietnamese soldiers. His grandfather hunted down and beheaded the rapists, but then fled to the mountains to hide. As a boy, Chantha would run food up into the mountains to sustain his fugitive grandfather. Growing up with these harsh realities, Chantha later joined the Cambodian military himself. During his military career, Chantha killed dozens of men.

But now, coming as a security guard and driver to a ministry seeking to care for girls rescued from trafficking, Chantha was one of the Mighty Men and the Holy Spirit was leading him to order his entire life according to God's Word. He felt called to be a pastor.

After much prayerful consideration we asked Chantha to be the pastor of our yet-to-be-launched Svay Pak church. Imagine how he must have felt. He knew God was calling him to be a pastor, but was he calling him to pastor in a village of mostly ethnic Vietnamese? Was God calling him to take his wife and newborn son from their comfortable home in the city of Phnom Penh and move them to a tiny apartment in the backwater village of Svay Pak where violence was a daily occurrence? He prayed. God said yes. Soon he and his family would move. Ratanak, our kids' club leader, would join him as the associate pastor.

## Launching the Svay Pak Church

In order to launch the church we needed a place to meet, a home for some of the church's ministries. At that time there were not many places residents were willing to make available to us. We decided the best option was the former brothel we were renting. The problem was that 80 percent of the building wasn't usable and the cost of renovating it was too high for a

## Chapter 10: Jesus Moves to Svay Pak

facility we didn't own. Through God's grace and provision we were able to buy the building. Renovation was a dirty task. As mentioned, there were snakes and rats, but they paled in comparison to the dark spirit that hung over the place. So with a group of volunteers we began renovations with a time of prayer, followed by days of demolition and restoration. There was an amazing physical and spiritual transformation.

We opened the church with the core ministries of a weekly worship service, daily walks through the community to build relationships, prayer, and discipleship. In addition, we continued the kids' club, and help to families in need of food. As we spent time in the community we would learn of other needs and would launch small ministries to meet those needs. They would all start very small, but would grow surprisingly fast. At some point they would grow beyond the time and ability of our expanding church staff and interfere with their primary responsibility to advance the kingdom of God in Svay Pak. As that happened, one by one, each became independent from the church, but always centered on Jesus Christ. They were always a conduit of his love and designed to draw people to him.

### Meeting Needs with Jesus' Love

It is not in the least an exaggeration to say a book could be written about each of these ministry programs. How God provided for each and how he transformed hundreds of lives through each adds up to thousands of stories. Since I want to finish this book sooner rather than later, I'll just share a little on why each ministry was launched, and offer a story of a life changed through it.

### Kids' Club

The kids' club continued with a few changes. First, it was expanded to five days a week, Monday through Friday. It grew from about thirty kids per day to over three hundred! I'd like to tell you it was the excellence of the program, but it wasn't. It would eventually become pretty good, but it wasn't in the beginning. So how did it grow? The story of Lexi provides the answer.

Lexi was one of the first children to attend our daily kids' club. She never missed a day. In spite of living in abject poverty, both materially and emotionally, she was full of energy, and participated in every activity. Over time as she experienced Jesus' love through the staff and learned about him through the daily lessons, she chose to make him her Savior and Lord. As Lexi was discipled by the staff she took on leadership roles at kids' club and eventually became the director. When short-term missions teams came to help she'd try to communicate with them, but it was difficult for her. So she asked if we would support her to attend English school. Our response was an enthusiastic "Yes!"

It didn't take Lexi very long to become quite fluent and share her story with visiting teams. One of the these teams, from a very large church, invited her to the States to share her story in front of the entire church. Bridget and I were invited to come along too. I was so fired up to hear Lexi share how the love of Jesus attracted her to the kids club and how he had, and was, working in her.

Bridget and I were a little nervous for Lexi as we walked with her to center stage and stood before hundreds of people. She was not. Her initial words surprised us.

"There was one thing I wanted when I walked into the kids' club, and it wasn't Jesus," she said. "I came for the snacks. I was hungry."

The church exploded with laughter. She went on to say, "But what I got was far better. I was loved more than ever before in my life. My family and the community didn't love me, they only loved what they could get from me. The staff told me the love I was getting came from Jesus. I knew I wanted to give this love to others. Now I am the leader of kids' club and I get to share his love every day!"

Laughter turned to tears.

A snack wrapped in Jesus' love transformed the heart of a child. Isn't that just like Jesus, meeting a felt need in order to open hearts to our most urgent need, a Savior.

Today every member of our kids' club leadership team are former attendees.

## Healthcare

Church attendance started to slowly increase as mothers saw the changes in their children who attended kids' club. It was rare that the fathers came along and participated. A need that came along with the moms and their kids was basic first aid, so we began a midweek clinic. It wasn't staffed with healthcare professionals, rather it was Bridget, Clay Butler (at that time a volunteer, today our CEO), and a few people from the church trained

## Chapter 10: Jesus Moves to Svay Pak

in first aid. The needs met were simple, like cleaning a cut, applying an antibiotic cream, and covering it with a Band-Aid. We also washed away lice, treated scabies, and handed out Tylenol. It gave us a chance to build relationships and pray for people. It's amazing what God can do through a couple of Tylenol.

One day an elderly women came in with a headache. Bridget gave her a couple of Tylenol to take right then, and a couple more to take later. The next day she returned headache free to thank Bridget and asked what she could do for her. Bridget said she had everything she needed, but it would be great if she came to Sunday service. The woman did, and kept coming back over the next several weeks. Each time she would hear about Jesus and how much he loves children and wants them protected.

About a month later she returned to the clinic, but this time with a much bigger problem. She walked up to Bridget and said, "I hear in church that Jesus loves children and wants them protected. Will your Jesus protect my granddaughter?"

With tears flowing and her body shaking she struggled to shared the story of her granddaughter, Wendy. She was nine years old.

Wendy, her mom, dad, and two siblings worked at one of the nine brick factories that surround Svay Pak. These were dangerous places to work for adults, let alone children. And they were not places of employment, but rather prisons for indentured servants.

Bricks cannot be made in the rainy seasons, as they are air dried before being fired in a kiln. During those times the workers had to borrow money from the factory owners to provide the basic necessities of life. During the dry season they wouldn't earn enough money to provide those necessities and pay back the loan. Every year they would fall further in debt. If a family's debt grew too big in comparison to the profit they generated, the owner would sell them to another brick factory.

Wendy and her family were sold for $700 to a brick factory in Kampong Thom, Cambodia, three hours away from Svay Pak. When the transfer was being made Wendy escaped and ran to her grandmother.

What seemed like a lucky break turned out to be a disaster. There were times when Wendy's grandmother would leave her alone while she did odd jobs to provide for the two of them. During those times, almost every time, men would rape nine-year-old Wendy without fear of repercussion.

Meeting the immediate need of keeping Wendy safe was really quite easy. After hearing the testimony of Wendy and her grandmother, and a report from the gynecologist who examined Wendy, the Cambodian government gave its approval for Wendy to enter our aftercare home. However, there's still more to the story.

Shortly after Wendy entered our home her father escaped from the brick factory and fled to Svay Pak and hid. The brick factory owner, having invested $700 to purchase this family, had lost the most productive part of the family and wanted him back. The owner gave Wendy's mom money for transportation to retrieve her husband. He made it clear they would never see their children again if they both didn't return. They chose not to return.

Once again Wendy's grandmother returned to the clinic. This time she asked if Jesus would save her grandchildren in Kampong Thom. Though reluctant, her daughter and son-in-law came along with her. We asked them to share all the details with our social worker assigned to Wendy's case. Armed with the details, she went to the police hoping they would rescue the kids. They said they wanted to help, but needed more evidence before they could conduct a raid to rescue the children.

Undeterred, our social worker took a bus to Kampong Thom and bravely snuck into the brick factory to secure the evidence the police needed. Shortly after the police conducted the raid and rescued the kids, but that wasn't all they did. During the raid they obtained further evidence, enough evidence to free all the enslaved people and arrest the brick factory owner.

Who knew a couple of Tylenol and the love of Jesus would lead to the freedom of so many?

Over the next couple of years the clinic expanded to a real healthcare clinic lead by an American doctor from Brazil who volunteered with us for over nine years. She was assisted by short-term medical missions teams who together would train up a Cambodian staff to run the clinic. As a result, hundreds of patients were cured physically and healed spiritually as they came to know Jesus as their Savior. And they became the protectors of children.

You may be wondering what happened to Wendy and the men who raped her. Sadly, it would be a few years before the men who raped women and children in Svay Pak were brought to justice. In the meantime, Wendy found healing and Jesus in our aftercare home. Later she would marry a good man and start a family whom she and her husband would faithfully love and protect.

## Chapter 10: Jesus Moves to Svay Pak

### Education

Another thing made evident through the kids' club was how few Svay Pak children were going to school. In some cases families wanted their children's help at home. Far more often it was a matter of finances; they couldn't afford to send their children to school. Public education was supposed to be free for grades one through twelve, but parents had to buy uniforms and teachers charged students a daily fee to receive instruction. For the families of Svay Pak living in abject poverty, education seemed like an unattainable dream. God would transform that unattainable dream into hope-filled reality through the AIM Christian School.

The vision for the school was initially small in size, kindergarten through grade three, but God-sized in purpose. That purpose was protection on three levels:

- **Immediate Protection** from traffickers and pedophiles through weekly visits by teachers and social workers.

- **Long-Term Protection** by providing the highest quality education in Cambodia, thus ending the cycle of poverty that plagued Svay Pak.

- **Eternal Protection** as the students come to know Jesus Christ as their Lord and Savior.

All we needed was a facility, equipment, books, supplies, a trained staff, and funding to pay their salaries. God provided a facility and funding through a Canadian NGO. The staffing, the most critical element, would not be as easy a need to fill. At that time there were not many well trained teachers in the area, who were Christians, and willing to teach in Svay Pak. How did we get over this hurdle?

The answer came through six expat long-term volunteers, LTVs. LTVs are individuals God calls to serve him through AIM in Cambodia. Long term means they are committed to serve a minimum of two years. The average stay is over five years, and some stay as long as ten years! They volunteer to work a regular forty-hour workweek, sharing their expertise and discipling our Cambodian staff so as to work themselves out of a job. In addition, they raise their own support. In the last eighteen years we have been blessed with thirty-four LTVs. Their volunteer service has saved us over $4 million in salaries.

The children's education included field trips that not only helped academically, but also included experiencing new things to expand their view of the world. Some field trips were just fun, like visiting the first Krispy Kreme franchise in Cambodia. One of the most impactful trips was to a brand new kids' discovery center in Phnom Penh. Not only did the kids learn a lot, they were given an unexpected opportunity.

The manager of the center approached the LTVs along on the trip and said, "Your kids should come back next week for the STEM [Science, Technology, Engineering, Math] contest sponsored by Prudential Company." The LTVs asked a few questions and found out there were twenty-four primary schools entered in the contest and the annual tuition for these school ran between $10,000 and $15,000. That's US dollars. These were the best schools in Cambodia and most of the students came from privileged backgrounds. In addition the contest was for fifth graders, and our kids were third graders. The LTVs decided the contest would likely cause more harm than good, and politely declined.

When the kids got back to Svay Pak the Cambodian teachers came to see school leadership. They knew about the STEM contest and all the details that went along with it and they still wanted their students to participate. They were proud of their students and would pray for God's protection. Hesitantly, the leadership agreed our students could participate.

It was definitely scary for the students as the contest began. First, the other students were wearing much nicer uniforms; second, the other students were twice their size. However, they did not stay intimidated. The contest lasted two long days and our students finished in second place, receiving silver medals and a cash prize for the school library!

The results bolstered the confidence of both the students and the teachers, and it did even more. The contest results were all over the Cambodian national media. The parents found new pride in sending their kids to school. The community pride grew, as did the parents' hope in what an education can provide. Suddenly, the applications to apply to our school began to increase. More children were eager to learn, and their parents wanted an education for them.

Soon our facility was maxed out with an enrollment of one hundred. We started to look for other places to rent and we ended up leasing five different buildings to house the school. It still wasn't enough space. Eventually, through God's miraculous provision we were able to build our own school with a capacity of fifteen hundred students.

Today the AIM school has an attendance of over six hundred and is slowly building its staffing to increase attendance. Some of the original students are attending university, others are AIM staff or have good and safe employment elsewhere. Every one of our students and their siblings have been protected from sex trafficking, and each one has learned who Jesus is.

*English School*

While the primary school grew, I began teaching an English class for young adults in our community. Hundreds of people signed up to take this English class—the big draw was that the course was being taught by an American. We accepted only twelve people for the class. I would teach them English, but I also partnered with Chantha, who would teach them about Jesus. All twelve are now leaders in AIM's ministry. Today over two hundred young adults attend English classes in our new facility where they also learn about Jesus.

And Chantha is using this experience to train other Cambodian pastors in making disciples. This is significant because we often see Cambodian churches strong on evangelism, but weak on discipleship. Chantha has become something like a Cambodian Rick Warren. People seek him out to be discipled by him. He is training a new generation of leaders for the Cambodian church. All of this has an impact on stabilizing neighborhoods so that trafficking can be more readily resisted.

It may seem that schools and a church could become a distraction from our mission of ending trafficking in Cambodia, but we see it as an essential aspect of what we're doing. Through the school, we are giving rescued girls and vulnerable kids in the community the opportunity for an academic education combined with the love of Jesus that is life-changing. We have never had a kid in the school become the victim of trafficking. This is at least in part due to the unannounced visits our social workers make to the families of our students. We make sure we know where the kids are and what their home life is like. The parents also realize that their kids are being cared for and invested in.

Now that we have a SWAT team, we also have the resources to rescue children who are trafficked. This is only the tip of the iceberg. These things help control behaviors out of fear, but lasting change comes from the transformation of hearts brought through the love of Jesus. Through this the school has had an enormous impact on trafficking prevention in Svay Pak.

I believe without a doubt the local church has the greatest impact on preventing trafficking. It has changed hearts one at a time to the point of community transformation. No longer is Svay Pak the epicenter of child sex trafficking; instead, it is a community that loves and protects its children, and all vulnerable people. And now they look beyond their own community to help children. One of my favorite Sundays at the Svay Pak church exemplified this truth.

The church took a special offering, in addition to weekly tithes and offerings, for Yemen. Pastor Chantha spoke to the church about kids in Yemen who were in great danger. The offering was about $80 US. I know this doesn't seem like much, but consider its source.

A community that has experienced brutal poverty for generations, a community known for selling its children, is now raising money to protect children on the other side of the world. What a beautiful thing!

I thought it couldn't get any better than that, but I was wrong. During the offering an elderly woman stood up and said, "I'm not going to let those kids go hungry. I give all the money I have. I don't care if I can't eat for a few days."

When she sat down another woman stood up and said, "No, you won't go hungry, you eat at my house this week." Now that's church!

That is what it looks like for the church to transform a community. When people function like this, caring for each other, pooling their resources, caring for others, and offering aid to people who find themselves going without, then the predatory lenders and traffickers can't get a foothold. Because Chantha answered God's call—allowing him to heal the pain and burdens of his past, following his leading and example, and choosing to heal the pain of others—Svay Pak, Cambodia, is functioning in a way that resists trafficking and offers life and hope to families and young girls.

We use other programs to prevent sex trafficking, but the premise is always the same: offer something to meet felt needs or desires of people in the community and when they come, use the opportunity to build relationships through which they can encounter Jesus and his love. Here are two examples that started as ministries of the church and grew to be independent ministries pointing to the church.

*Young Adult Discipleship*

Cambodia has national scholastic tests after sixth, ninth, and twelfth grades. Each of these milestones are rightly considered huge accomplishments in

## Chapter 10: Jesus Moves to Svay Pak

this society, but for this reason we often have kids dropping out of school after ninth grade. The families don't see the value of the additional three years. We've created a discipleship program that allows young men and women to exit their home situations and focus on their studies for three years so they can hit that twelfth-grade milestone. They get up early, do their devotions, finish their schoolwork, and volunteer in some of our ministry programs after school. All of this includes outreach to the community and it allows the girls to gain more resilience from the societal pressures that so often result in trafficking.

## Employment

Good, safe employment is a need both rescued and vulnerable young women need. It helps keep them away from the hands of traffickers. The employment we offer is both good and safe, and comes with Jesus' love. Once again this program was not started as part of well thought out strategic planning; it was birthed out of meeting a need of one girl that grew to helping several hundred.

### *AIM Employment Center*

One day as Bridget and I were standing outside of the church in Svay Pak, two sisters came to us asking for help. They shared how they were trafficked by their mother to pay off a debt, and after they were raped by multiple men every day for months the debt was paid and they returned home. Overjoyed to be free, they set out helping their mother and younger siblings. However, the joy was short-lived; their mother had racked up more debt. Harassed by those she owed, their mother let her children know they would soon be sold again. The girls asked us to please pay off the loans.

We wanted to help the girls, but knew paying off the loans was not the answer. I had always wanted to provide good, safe employment to rescued girls and those at risk, but that alone would not be enough in this case. The loans that needed paying were with neighborhood loan sharks and at crazy interest rates. The girls' mother was making some payments, but with the high interest rate the debt was getting bigger, not smaller. The first step was to get those interest rates reduced and set up a reasonable plan to pay off the loans. To that end we met with the three "lenders."

I was a little anxious about meeting with them, maybe even a little scared, but what I soon found out they was were more afraid of me than I was of them. They weren't used to negotiating with a big white guy. Making a long story short, each agreed to a monthly payback plan without any more interest, as long as we hired the girls and did payroll deductions. I agreed. Now all we needed were jobs for the girls.

I thought we had the answer. The girls could make hand-quilted pillowcases from Cambodian silk. This would not only help them, but those who made the silk. The idea wasn't mine; two senior ladies, Judy Sisneros and Susie Ernst, who were quilting experts had volunteered to come to Cambodia to train our girls. These ladies were called on to persevere through culture shock and the dirty village of Svay Pak for several months in order to train the girls to make a high-quality product.

They were over-the-top successful. The girls became artisans producing incredibly beautiful pillowcases. Before we knew it they had made over three thousand pillowcases! Sadly, we had only sold six. One of my degrees is in marketing. I should have know a great product without distribution, in the end, is a failure. Once again God had us covered. He provided two successful businesspeople, Ken Petersen and Jen Bulotti, to help in product development and distribution. They even started their own company to sell products the girls produce. It's still in operation today under the name Noble Venture. You can check it out at www.noble-venture.com.

Over time the girls were producing jewelry and clothing, especially T-shirts for churches and other organizations. And they were selling. What the girls made could be bought for less, but with the products the girls made you bought more... you bought *freedom* for the girl who made it.

Best of all the girls do not just have a good, safe job, they receive training and education for a future dream job. They are discipled to find a purpose beyond themselves while daily experiencing Jesus' love.

Since all the income for the sale of products is put back into the girls and their jobs, the employment center has grown from helping a few girls to a few hundred. Prior to the pandemic, annual sales were just under $800,000. As important as those numbers are, they pale in comparison to a single heart and life transformed. Here's how one of the girls described her experience.

"Hello, my name is Edith. I work at the AIM Employment Center. I make shirts and bracelets. I have been working here for three years. Before I had this job here I felt like I was worthless. I was a bad woman, and when

## Chapter 10: Jesus Moves to Svay Pak

I came here everyone welcomed me and loved me. When I came here I felt like a princess. This organization, this employment center, when we are in need, they always support us."

While Edith worked in our employment center she grew in her relationship with Jesus and decided she wanted to be used by God to help other girls. She studied and took specialized training, and today she is a teacher in our school. She is sharing the welcome and love of Jesus she experienced at the employment center while preparing children to break the cycle of poverty that enslaves their families. Edith is just one of the many former victims who are modern-day abolitionists.

The recent COVID pandemic was particularly tough on the employment center as the Cambodian government shut down the country for two years. Unable to produce products, our sales plummeted to zero, while the girls' need for a stable income grew. As has happened many times in the history of AIM, God provided, so we were able to pay the girls a salary every month through the shutdown. Today (February 2023) we are in the process of winning back customers with a vision to grow so we can continue providing employment for more girls.

### *The Lord's Gym*

At this point we were touching every segment of the Svay Pak community except one, the young men who trafficked and abused girls. Knowing the horrific damage these young men were doing to the girls and the community, my gut response was to reach them with a baseball bat. It was hard to imagine the truth that God loved these young men; he loved them as much as the girls they were abusing. So the question became, how can we reach them with the transformational love of Jesus? None of our current programs offered anything they wanted. One day the idea came to me . . . the Lord's Gym!

The gym started out with a focus on weight lifting. Two members of Radical Reality, Terry and Dean, from the Lord's Gym in Roseville, California, came to Cambodia to launch Svay Pak's Lord's Gym. Radical Reality visits high schools throughout the United States performing feats of strength in order to have the opportunity to share Jesus with the students and what really makes a man strong. It would be the same in Svay Pak, except they would walk around the village doing small examples of their strength to entice people to come to the gym's grand opening.

Terry and Dean probably didn't need to do more than walk around because they were the biggest men anyone in the village had ever seen. The biggest by a long shot! I loved the reaction they'd get when they picked up a frying pan and rolled it up like a burrito.

The walkabout worked and almost one hundred people, mostly young men, showed up for the grand opening. Terry and Dean performed feats of strength, shared the gospel, and invited everyone to come back the next day to work out with them. Around fifty young men showed up the next day and continued coming every day for the two weeks Terry and Dean were there. Our church pastor, Chantha, was there as well. He translated for the guys as they trained the young men in weight lifting techniques and talked about true strength in Jesus Christ. They also encouraged the men to attend church, where a few gave their lives to Christ. Whether they came to church or not, they learned about Jesus and his love for them every day at the gym. Some chose to put their faith in Jesus and no longer traffic or abuse women and children.

After Terry and Dean returned home, attendance at the gym dropped by half. God was using the gym and lives were being changed, but it wasn't growing. Spurts of growth would happen when Terry and Dean returned each year, but would slow down when they returned home.

That changed one day when Coach Bird came to the gym looking for a job. Coach Bird brought two things with him: a love of Jesus and, as a former national champion, expertise in kickboxing. Kickboxing is the biggest sport in Cambodia. Fights are televised every week and the champions become real-life heroes.

With the addition of Coach Bird many more young men began attending the gym, including one who was considered the baddest man in Svay Pak. He trafficked and abused drugs and girls. He was considered beyond help, but one day he showed up at they gym. Coach mentored him in boxing and showed him Jesus. He began to turn his life around and he became one hell of a boxer. In a relatively short time he became the undefeated national champion, which came with a trophy and $3,000. He shared that money with his family and the gym.

The gym exploded; dozens of young men came to join. In just a few years the gym had three national champions, had moved from its tiny cramped quarters to a state-of-the-art gym, and was named one of the top gyms in the country by the Cambodian National Boxing Association. That sounds like great news, but it wasn't.

## Chapter 10: Jesus Moves to Svay Pak

Worldly success had gotten us off-mission. Our mission for Jesus to transform abusers of women and children to be their protectors had become secondary to building national champions. By God's grace transformation was taking place, but it became a secondary measurement. The gym that was built for the young men of Svay Pak became filled with men from all over Cambodia; the stories we told were about national champions, and the stories of average boxers who became godly men were not.

Thank God today that has changed as one of those untold stories has become the new coach. Hokchin, born and raised in Svay Pak, was an above-average boxer, the hardest worker in the gym, but a series of concussions forced him to quit boxing. That's something that could have weakened his faith, but his grew. He continued to attend Bible studies and church services, growing in his faith. He became one of our security guards and the people he protected saw Jesus in him. One of those people was our granddaughter Lexi, who spent a summer with us. She was amazed at how gentle, yet effective, he was in quelling any conflict that arose. He was redefining what it meant to be a strong man.

Today, Hokchin has returned the gym to its original purpose. He's not only working with the young men of Svay Pak, but has initiated programs for young women, boys, and girls. No national champions yet, but who cares!

### Behavior Change vs. Transformation

Transformation isn't immediate, it takes time, sometimes a long time. For that reason we have found many ways to enforce behavior change during the transformation process. For example, when we learned that spousal abuse was rampant, we prayerfully considered what meaningful action we could take. We came up with the idea that when a husband abused his wife for the first time, we would go to the home with the police and have him sign a contract stating that if he did it again he'd have to go to prison. Simple as that sounds, it worked! It was amazing.

We used the same process for reintegrating girls into society, especially the older ones. As I've already explained, so many of the girls who are trafficked carry an immense culturally imposed burden to care for their families. We found that even girls who were rescued and healed could end up back in the brothels when their families guilted them into earning significant money to support their family. Obviously this arrangement helps no one and only perpetuates the evils that have been destroying the souls of these girls and the society as a whole. So when we were ready to send a girl back into society, we would have the family come to the police station to sign a contract stating that if on our regular check-ins we can't find their daughter—that if the daughter ended up being trafficked again—then the family would be the ones going to prison. The police were happy to partner with us in this and it has proven to be a way to bring some behavior change to the local neighborhoods and safety for the girls.

## WHERE DOES JESUS LIVE?

I know, in your heart. That's true, but it's not what I mean. My question is: Where are we planting churches? Where are we supporting church plants? While there are some exceptions, the overwhelming number of churches are being planted in suburbia. This seems contrary to where the greatest need lies: cities. It's in the cities we find the greatest concentration of evil and poverty, the greatest opportunity to transform our world. The Apostle Paul left us the example of church planting in urban areas. Jesus describes the church as prevailing over the gates of hell. The gates of hell may protect places of evil, but they are no match for the church as an offensive weapon.

Don't get me wrong, planting a church in the midst of evil requires facing danger and perseverance, and of course faith, hope, and love. On the other hand, finding ways to meet people's felt needs in order to build a relationship leading to Jesus is easier. One thing is for sure, if we live with Jesus in the midst of such blatant evil there's no way to look away.

# CHAPTER 11: GOING BACK

## PERSEVERING LOVE

OVER THE YEARS, WE have developed simple programs to meet easily recognizable needs that have been far more effective in the battle against sex trafficking than we ever imagined. But from the very beginning, we knew that programs were never going to be the key to success. What we've found is that people are the key in the battle against human trafficking. More specifically, we have found that Jesus and his church have been the key to transforming the hearts of people into modern-day abolitionists.

From the moment we started the little church in Svay Pak it provided all of the crucial intel that freed Carol. Initially our SWAT team and the Cambodian police counted on the intel that came from everyday church members, those who took the time to be observant and to report what they saw—not for personal gain, but because the love of Jesus compelled them to love their neighbors as themselves. Our SWAT team has since developed an intel network across the entire country, but it all started with the church.

This is a powerful reminder that God uses simple and seemingly insignificant people to overpower seemingly insurmountable strongholds.

We find again and again that the most powerful force God uses is unconditional love. This is especially true in the healing process, as we work with the girls who have been rescued and healed and help them build a thriving life in their communities. There are many factors that go into this process, but it simply could not be done without persevering and unconditional love.

Almost all the girls who have been sold into sex slavery have never experienced true love from their families. One of our core commitments is to embody love for the girls through every step of the process. When the girls come to our restoration homes, we use cutting edge therapy to help them process and heal. This is absolutely vital. But it is cognitive, it deals with the head. It can bring a girl from victim to survivor, but falls short of God's (and our) desire that each girl will thrive.

What takes a girl from surviving to thriving is Jesus' unconditional love they receive from our team throughout their lives. In every case, the girls who come to us have been taught through words and actions that they are trash. This is reinforced by the Cambodian proverb that says, "Men are like gold. Women are like white cloth; once soiled by mud, it can be washed but never made clean again." After their families have sold them and their captors have abused them, these girls believe it at a deep level.

Therapy teaches the girls that they are valuable and lovable. But the transformation doesn't take place until they experience being valued and loved. Words alone don't lead to thriving. Our therapists do a phenomenal job of preparing the girls to live with our house moms, and then in this home environment they experience the reality of being valued and loved. In essence, they are experiencing what the church is all about: a community shaped by the love of Christ that flows to each person and through each person. The problem is that in our flesh, none of us has enough love for these girls. We all run dry at some point. As I have mentioned, because of the severe abuse the girls have experienced they can be difficult, and their need for love overwhelming. Personally, my human love would run out at about 9 AM daily. It's not that I don't care, it's just that the well runs dry.

The miracle that we experience in Christ, however, is that his love flows through us: "We love because he first loved us" (1 John 4:19). Paul compares the working of God's Spirit in our lives to fruit growing on a tree. It's not something we work hard to conjure up or sustain. By virtue of the Spirit working within us, fruit grows in our lives. And that fruit, Paul tells us, looks like "love, joy, peace, patience, kindness, goodness, faithfulness, gentleness, and self-control" (Gal 5:22–23). In other words, the things we most need in order to love these girls well are the very things that God himself promises to supernaturally produce in our lives. An environment in which this kind of fruit miraculously grows in abundance is an environment in which real transformation can take place. Each one of us must be careful to maintain our connection to Jesus: when we do this the well never runs dry.

It is amazing to watch our house moms love these girls so well while they're in our care. And once we send them back to work in the community,

## Chapter 11: Going Back

our social workers continue that love to the girls by checking in every month with every girl. As each girl reenters society, she knows she's remembered. She continues to experience unconditional love and be discipled. Once, one of our girls decided to go back to a brothel, so our social workers continued to follow up with her in the brothel. She was not forgotten or dismissed even when she chose to reenter hell. Through that continued love, this girl eventually decided to leave the brothel and allowed us to guide her into a thriving life.

## JUNE

The story you are about to read will seem unbelievable or hyperbolic. It's not. It's a story we'd like to look away from. It makes us angry and sad. As June told me her story she showed little emotion, like this is just the way life is. She asked me why my eyes welled with tears.

When June was five years old, she was sold by her mother to a rich family in Phnom Penh to be a household slave. This was different than being sold as a sex slave, but it's still slavery. Once a year, June would get a visit from her mother when she came to collect the money she "earned" by her daughter's labor. Apart from those short and unaffectionate visits, June had no relationship with her mother or the rest of her family.

June was never allowed out of the house. Imagine being this five-year-old girl, coming from a rural setting into a city with close to two million people, but not knowing a single one of them. She could hear all the foreign and scary noises of the city, but had no idea what they were. Her entire world was reduced to a single house, a house in which she performed duties meant for an adult. She never set foot in a school.

Even though she was sold as a household slave, as she neared puberty, the men in the house wanted to have sex with her. When one of the boys in the house tried to rape her, she ran away. Somehow, June found her way back to her family, believing that if she explained the situation, they'd be as upset as her and welcome her home. Instead, they told her, "You need to get us money. We don't care how you do it, just go back to Phnom Penh and make money to send home."

With no options, June went back to the city and went about trying to find a job. As she wandered around the city a man on a moto asked her if she was lost and needed help. She explained that she needed work and he told her he could help. He took her to a message parlor where she was offered a job as a cleaner.

She took the job, but soon discovered that the massage parlor functioned as a brothel, and her "employers" were grooming her to be sold for sex. This became her new existence, sold for sex as many as twenty times a day. For all this abuse she earned a few dollars to send to her family, and the brothel owner got rich. One day as she sat out in front of the massage parlor, a drunk driver in a SUV ran her over and ripped off one of her legs. She remembers before passing out that she could see her leg lying in front of the brothel as she was rushed to the hospital. When she woke up after surgery she wasn't surprised that she no longer had two legs, only one.

When she was finally discharged from the hospital, June returned home to her family again. They gave her a couple of weeks for her wound to heal and then told her that she had to go back to the brothel. After the "respite" of her hospital and recovery time, June's life went back to what it was, except that now she had to hop on one leg everywhere she went.

Eventually, our SWAT team made a raid that rescued June from the brothel. When our team recovered the records, we discovered that she was the most "popular" girl in the brothel due to the loss of her leg, which means that she was selected to be raped more often than any of the other girls. Because June was around twenty years old at the time, she didn't have to come to our aftercare facility, but she chose to enter our program. We weren't sure how it would work; she was the oldest girl to come into our home.

June was incredible. We got her a prosthetic leg, took her through therapy, and she had a real encounter with Jesus. Almost immediately she began to share love she was receiving with the staff and other girls. She became the best kind of big sister to many girls. We rejoiced as a staff over how God was working in her life.

While June was at our home, she was trained on making hand-spun yarn by a company out of Hong Kong. They were planning on opening a facility in Phnom Penh providing employment for over one hundred of our girls. June was paving the way and was doing an amazing job!

## WORK

At that time, when we reintegrated girls into society, we couldn't always have jobs lined up for them outside of our restoration homes. We didn't

## Chapter 11: Going Back

realize what a short time we had to find good employment before girls like June would feel compelled to return to the brothels. The economic pull is too strong and the societal forces that have trained these girls to fall into this oppressive system are too finely tuned. Our experience was primarily with younger girls with whom we had more time to educate and find good employment.

The Hong Kong company we were counting on decided not to move forward with the project, so the job June was trained for wasn't there. We were too slow in finding other employment. June got rid of the prosthetic leg we had gotten for her and stopped responding to our social workers who continued to reach out to her. We told her that she didn't need to work in the brothel, that we would set her up to do yarn spinning from her own home, but it was too late. Bridget tried several times to follow up and let her know we loved her and coax her out, but we were unsuccessful

Eventually, June left for another brothel and we lost our ability to contact her. From that moment on we didn't know where she was, but we found out she was recruiting other girls to join her in the brothel. Tragically, this trafficked girl had become a trafficker herself. Our failure haunts me to this day. June is permanently on my prayer list.

My hope is found in Isaiah 55:10-11: "As the rain and the snow come down from heaven, and do not return to it without watering the earth and making it bud and flourish, so that it yields seed for the sower and bread for the eater, so is my word that goes out from my mouth: It will not return to me empty, but will accomplish what I desire and achieve the purpose for which I sent it."

This story is tragic, and we realized that we couldn't let it happen again. We have found that when we reintegrate someone with a good job and continue to follow up with them, we have a 100 percent success rate at keeping them from returning to the sex trade. We have also learned that solid jobs are essential for successful reintegration. And with that, we found another aspect of our work in Cambodia that needed to be developed.

There are very few jobs that provide these girls with enough money to support themselves and their families. In reality, both aspects are necessary in Cambodian society. We've mentioned girls "choosing" to go back to the brothels when they can't make enough money elsewhere. It's true that they make this decision sometimes, but it's not really accurate to call it a choice.

In Cambodia, there is no social security, and every child knows that there will come a time when their parents are no longer able to work. There is enormous pressure to find a way to earn enough money to support their parents. There is something beautiful about grown kids caring for their aging parents, but with all of the dynamics involved, it only makes the problems of trafficking worse.

In the most terrible cases, parents that are able to work choose to sell their kids so they don't have to get a job. But even for families with working parents, many kids have to "choose" between working in a brothel or not making enough money for themselves to live on—to say nothing of their families—in a society with no social security, no healthcare, lacking in basic human rights, and in which food and shelter are often difficult to secure. That's really not a choice. On top of that, most of the cases we see are with minors working in brothels, which means that the word "choice" does not apply at all.

The girls in our aftercare facilities generally fall into two categories. Because of our educational programs, the girls that come to us between eight and eleven years old actually have an opportunity to graduate from high school, which means it's possible for them to go to university, gain English skills, and get a shot at one of the few jobs that can actually provide a reasonable living. Then we have girls who arrive between twelve and sixteen years old. These "older" girls have never been to school, and they're very unlikely to graduate high school. Most of the time, these girls are frustrated by our attempts at schooling them. Those girls have very little opportunity to find a job that will provide enough to keep them safe.

## THE EMPLOYMENT CENTER

You read about our employment center in chapter 9. June's story emphasizes how critical it is for many of the girls to live a life of thriving. What follows are a few more things about the center you should know.

If you look at it logically, we hire the very worst employees available at the employment center with hope that through mentoring and discipleship they will become outstanding employees. Most are illiterate. They have no experience that would create a good work ethic. And our business model is not geared toward maximizing profit. The products the girls make cost more than the competition's because we pay well and offer healthcare and childcare. We also require (and pay) every employee to continue their education while they work for us. A significant number of girls would rather not get paid to do this and instead do their regular job—that's how much they

## Chapter 11: Going Back

hate school—but we see it as an opportunity to help them move beyond our employment centers. In addition, we work on the soft skills that will make them better employees wherever they work. Another important part of our employment center . . . let me rephrase that . . . *the* most important part of our employment center is the continuing discipleship of the girls.

## MUCH MORE

We're certain this is not the end of the story. At every stage, we're struck by how much more work there is to do than we imagined. We never thought it would be easy—after all, trafficking is a massive, multifaceted evil that has plagued humanity throughout history. But on the other hand, we left for Cambodia believing that if we could simply take care of some of the girls who were being rescued from sex slavery, then we would be fulfilling everything God had in store for us. As you now know, that has expanded to gathering intelligence on trafficking operations, launching a SWAT team, developing employment centers, and much more. As you'll see in the next chapter, God has had still more in store for us.

All of it has been about the good of these girls. But as we found out, it's also been about the good of Cambodia and the rest of the world. It's also been about our own good. We've learned that trusting God is a far richer concept than we could have imagined. We've been reminded again and again that he can do the impossible. Perhaps most surprisingly, we have learned that we can do the impossible because God chooses to empower us for the amazing things he wants to do in the world.

## LOOK THIS WAY

A way of not looking away is looking for, and purchasing ethically made products. There are a number of good choices, but I'm focusing on the products our girls produce. All you need to do to find other products is Google "ethically made products." Our girls produce great jewelry and garments. To purchase something for yourself or a gift for others all you have to do is shop AIM Apparel at https://aimapparel.org/. You'll be taking a first step in becoming a modern-day abolitionist, bringing freedom to the girl who made the product, and getting a great product on top of it. Every product purchased comes with a tag signed by the girl who made it. You can put the tag on your refrigerator, bathroom mirror, or some other place as a reminder to pray for her.

I'm hoping you'll go a step further as an advocate for the groups you belong to and purchase their custom tees and polo shirts from AIM. Churches, schools, companies, and all sorts of other organizations routinely buy T-shirts and polo shirts, and much of the time they are not ethically made. Check out our website, https://www.aimcustom.org/aimcustom/shop/home, and see how easy it is to get the custom tee you desire.

The best thing is, whether you are buying a personal item or custom tees or polo shirts for a group you belong to, freedom comes with every item!

# CHAPTER 12: FIGHTING BACK

## LINDA

When we first met Linda, she entered our restoration program as a little girl who had a broken arm that had never healed properly. This gave her a slight physical disability, which lowers a girl's already low chances of success in Cambodia. Making things worse, Linda's mother was a child sex trafficker. As Linda neared puberty her mother sold her along with a dozen other girls. After a hellish time in sex slavery, Linda was rescued and brought to our restoration home, where she began to experience the love and care of our house moms.

One of the things that most struck me about Linda was her love for the Bible. Her house mom taught her 1 Corinthians 13, and Linda decided to memorize the whole chapter and recite it for everyone. It was a moving experience to hear a little girl who has experienced so much evil stand and joyfully proclaim that, "love is patient, love is kind. It does not envy, it does not boast, it is not proud. It does not dishonor others, it is not self-seeking, it is not easily angered, it keeps no record of wrongs. Love does not delight in evil but rejoices with the truth. It protects, always trusts, always hopes, always perseveres. Love never fails." She could joyfully proclaim it because she had experienced that kind of love. She convicted me and inspired me to do better in memorizing Scripture. I started with 1 Corinthians 13.

Shortly after Linda's rescue her mother was put in prison for trafficking little girls. In Cambodia, a mother can choose to take her children with her into prison; some do it because they have no one to watch their children and they might be left on the street. Others choose to bring them for the money. Due to the harsh conditions in Cambodian prisons, some Western

NGOs provide financial support for the incarcerated. A prisoner receives more support if she has a child with her. Linda's mother did it for the money.

Linda wasn't the only girl in our care who had a mother in prison. Each month we would take all those girls to visit their mothers who were serving time. Each girl was provided with food, water, and some toiletries to give their mothers.

When Linda began visiting her mother, she found out her younger brother was living in the prison as well. Her heart was broken by a combination of fear and compassion. Fear because the prison was co-ed and contained those imprisoned for everything from a minor misdemeanor to rape and murder. Compassion because this little girl who had survived so much was so full of love that she wanted to give her younger brother the better life she was living.

Month after month Linda would visit her mom in prison and with tears rolling down her cheeks begged her mother to let her take her brother home with her. The answer was always, "No!"

Even though she was told "no" so many times Linda continued to visit her mom in prison and beg for her brother's freedom after she was reintegrated back into her community. She had secured a good job with one of our partner organizations so she could be responsible for his care. Her persevering love and prayers did not fail. Her mother finally agreed to let her brother leave the prison and live with his sister. Linda was thrilled. She functioned as a mother to her younger brother, overflowing in the love of Jesus neither of them had ever received from their family. But her love didn't stop there. Linda lived in a shack of a house in a poor community surrounded by kids who weren't able to go to school. She wanted to help these kids. So every day, when she would get home from work, Linda invited the kids to her tiny home and taught them to read and write. She used a little of the money she earned from her job to buy pencils, notebooks, and textbooks for the kids.

Eventually, Linda got married and now has her own children. (Read more of her story in Appendix 2.) She is more than a survivor. Linda is a modern-day abolitionist. This is the real healing: when a girl has experienced true love and is compelled to offer that love to the people around her. We didn't teach Linda to help the kids in her community; she did it spontaneously out of the overflow of a heart that truly believed that love always protects, always trusts, always hopes, always perseveres.

## Chapter 12: Fighting Back

There is so much more to the healing process than helping these girls deal with their trauma, though of course that is vital. Our true goal is to send these girls back into society to flourish there. But there's actually more to it than that.

Very often, we've seen these girls turn into more than survivors, as true and important as it is that they are survivors. What we've seen over and over is girls turning into badasses who dive back into their communities and become abolitionists in big and small ways. They appear to be fearless as they bravely step into the very communities that discarded and enslaved them. They make these communities safer. They fill the streets and schools with love. They provide protection and opportunity for kids to be kids and to grow into flourishing adults.

I am so thankful for the way that God has used our staff, expat volunteers, supporters, Bridget, and me in combating an evil that can seem impossible to overcome. Through us, God has rescued young girls that wicked people tried to trample into oblivion and then used them as some of the most powerful and specialized abolitionists this world has ever seen. Sometimes that has looked like Linda lovingly teaching the kids in her own community. Other times it looks like Betty, whom you met in the introduction and in chapter 4, attacking the trafficking industry head-on.

## THE DECISION

If you recall what I shared about Betty in earlier chapters, she was one of our toughest cases in the aftercare home. She proved to be too difficult for other organizations and, because of that, she was God's answer to our prayer that he send us the most difficult cases, the ones no one else wanted. I have already shared that through the long perseverance of the house moms, Betty began to not just hear us tell her that she was loved, valued, and special—she began to believe it. It took real human beings proving to her every single day that they loved her for Betty to begin to see herself as lovable. And that changed everything.

Towards the end of her restoration process, Betty got it into her head that she wanted to go to America to study. This is very difficult for these girls to do because they are so behind in their studies and have countless other obstacles to overcome. But Betty wanted to try. We told her that if she could pass a US GED test online, we would have a pretty good chance of getting her into a college program in America. Betty took this as a challenge and started studying immediately. We were even able to get an expat to come to Cambodia to work with her one on one for an entire year!

As Betty dug deeper and deeper into her studies, she began to realize that it would take another year or two before she was ready for the exam. She was getting tired of her studies and began to get restless. She wanted to do something! We weren't surprised when she told us she wanted to change course, but her choice was powerful. She told us:

"I want to be able to help other girls."

It was the love of Jesus that had transformed Betty's life. Now it was the love of Jesus that was compelling her to offer life-transforming love to other people in her community: "No one has greater love than this: to lay down his life for his friends" (John 15:13). When Betty told us she wanted to help other girls, we were seeing firsthand the power of persevering love.

The love that had transformed her was now compelling her to go outward. This is always the trajectory of true love.

## ABOLITIONIST

Once her decision was made, Betty began working as a trainee at our transitional home for girls rescued from trafficking in Siem Reap, Cambodia. She went to work sharing the hope in her story to convince the rescued girls that there was great hope for them. But Betty wasn't content to stay in the transitional home. She wanted to find the girls that were still trapped! She wanted to go directly to them.

Though a lot of trafficking operations function underground, many are still out in the open. Many "KTVs" (karaoke clubs) and beer gardens are scantily disguised brothels. Everyone knows what goes on just behind the scenes; it's an open secret. Betty began walking directly into these publicly known brothels and clubs where girls were being pimped and sold.

The "older" girls who are in these places aren't typically being physically restrained. But don't think they're not imprisoned. What is happening in these settings is that these girls have been abused so persistently for so long that they themselves begin to believe that they aren't good for anything else. They're trained to believe that their families need them to do this kind of work, that they'll never succeed at anything else, and that they don't have any other value. As I've been saying throughout this book, these chains are stronger than steel. They are carefully crafted with fear, shame, and poverty and they prove extremely effective in the perpetuation of evil.

## Chapter 12: Fighting Back

These are the types of invisible chains that hold these girls in slavery. This is why Betty's task is so impossibly difficult. She has to speak to girls raised in this culture, many times betrayed and discarded by their own families, violated by traffickers, pimps, and johns, and convince them that there is a new life waiting for them. Convince them they are special.

Betty walks into these dark places in the middle of the day (when the girls aren't busy "working") and attempts what we call assisted self-rescues. I assure you that this is far more difficult than what our SWAT team does. Forcing our way past traffickers and running out with girls under our arms is easier than convincing these "older" girls that there is another life waiting for them outside their unguarded prison.

When Betty goes to talk to these girls in the brothels, she shares her own story with them. She tells them that they can leave today and be taken to a place where they can live and be safe. She tells them that there are jobs for them where they can earn enough money to care for themselves and help support their families. As good as that sounds, Betty is unlikely to convince a girl on her first visit. Despite the challenges she keeps going back and investing in a relationship with each girl. She proves to them that she cares for them beyond a onetime gesture.

There are other well-intentioned groups that will come and show kindness to the girls by bringing a rose and a bag of toiletries. It's a nice gesture meant to affirm their value, but the girls know that once they've received their rose and gift bag, they'll never see anyone from that group again. It doesn't do anything to show these girls—who have been taught never to trust anyone—that there is someone on the outside who truly loves them. Betty, on the other hand, is willing to keep going back as long as each girl is willing to meet with her.

Once a girl expresses some interest, Betty will bring her to see the aftercare home. She shows her the place that could be her home. She's shown there are jobs available for her.

As I said, Betty is excellent at this. She used to manipulate people for her survival. Now she uses her charm to win people over for a godly purpose. While not every girl responds well to Betty's efforts, she has drawn more girls than we're able to care for with our current capabilities. As I'm writing this, we have a waiting list of seventy girls that Betty has reached that we don't have the resources to place yet.

In the midst of all of this, Betty became part of a church and met an amazing young man who was serving as the equivalent of a youth pastor.

They fell in love, and I was honored to officiate Betty's wedding. I sobbed through the whole thing. After they had been married for a while, they had their first child. At the same time, Betty's sister, who had two kids, buckled under drug addiction and was not able to care for her children. She wasn't able to get into any programs that would help with her kids, so shortly after having their first baby, Betty and her husband welcomed their two nieces into their home, where they cared for these children as their own until her sister got straight. From being trafficked as a child to providing the persistent, unconditional love that other children need to have for hope of a real future, Betty's story is a reminder that God uses people the world thinks least likely to do the impossible.

Every one of these victims-turned-survivors-turned-abolitionists is a reminder that evil cannot win in the end. As powerful as evil feels—and trust me, this work shows just how powerful evil can be—God is bigger. Though evil often seems to claim an irreversible hold on a person or a place, what Paul said to the Romans is true for all of us: "The God of peace will soon crush Satan under your feet" (Rom 16:20).

Paul knew how powerful evil could be, and in the Letter to the Romans he was addressing people whose lives were affected by that evil. He knew that our tendency is to see evil as the most powerful force available, which is why we are often drawn towards the power of darkness even as we seek to fight against it. Paul's statement reminds us that evil is not nearly as powerful as it seems: "Do not be overcome by evil, but overcome evil with good" (Rom 12:21).

As terrifying as evil can be, we always need to remember John's words: "There is no fear in love, but perfect love casts out fear" (1 John 4:18).

What is stronger than evil and fear and Satan? Love and goodness and the God of peace.

As someone who has seen unimaginable evil up close, I understand why evil and fear are so intimidating. But these girls have shown me that love and goodness are actually more powerful. The evils of trafficking and sexual predation and the pornography industry have crushed so many lives. But I've seen love resurrect hearts that we thought were dead. We have seen the unconditional love of our house moms give these girls a new life, but also strengthened with the resolve, maturity, and wisdom that only comes from traveling the hard path. And I have watched the unconditional love that these girls have received and then in the lives of others as they continue the battle against the evil of human trafficking.

## Chapter 12: Fighting Back

**A WORD OF CAUTION**

As I tell stories of amazing transformation, I want you to know *"it's not love a girl for awhile, she's transformed, and from then on her life is perfect."* Their lives after transformation are just like ours, filled with ups and downs, successes and failures, gains and losses. Just like us they need to be loved and supported through the downs, and cheered and encouraged through the ups. Just like us, they need a family of believers. The fact that their lives can become just like ours is a miracle!

The need of love, support, and encouragement for the victims of child sex trafficking is evident. Conversely, the same need is often hidden in the people who daily cross our paths. I know I need to be a better with friends and strangers walking in and out of my life. How about you? I'm pretty confident love, support, and encouragement are never wasted.

# CHAPTER 13: CONFLICT

It all began when CNN did a couple of documentaries on child sex trafficking in Cambodia that featured our work. Great news, right? The documentaries would build awareness of sex trafficking and our work to combat it. As a result, there would be more people joining the fight and more support for AIM. Both of those results were achieved, but that wasn't all it achieved.

**PARTNER CONFLICT**

First, I highly recommend you don't have any partner conflict. Second, partner conflict is probably unavoidable unless you choose to do nothing, choose to look away. Our partner conflict was with a very close partner, one we greatly admired. The conflict began after CNN aired a fifty-minute documentary, *Every Day in Cambodia*, in May 2015. The documentary focused on three Svay Pak girls who were sex trafficked, rescued, and beginning their new life of freedom. It included our involvement in their stories.

Our partner felt the documentary exaggerated the extent of child sex trafficking in Svay Pak and in Cambodia. In response they wrote an op-ed piece that was printed in *The Washington Post*. The article spoke of progress made, which was certainly true, progress had been made. However, there were statements presented as facts that I disagreed with, and one sentence around which the article was formed angered me . . .

> The truth is that the Cambodian police dropped the hammer on the criminals who buy and sell little girls and have virtually *obliterated* the crime from the kingdom.

Angered, I responded by writing my own op-ed piece and sent it to *The Washington Post*. They printed it. In the article I went point by point

# Chapter 13: Conflict

refuting what was said by our partner, even quoting Cambodian government officials to support my position. My closing statement criticized our partner . . .

> Decrying "mission accomplished" in the fight against child sex trafficking in Cambodia is premature. The danger in doing this too soon is that, by exaggerating the success, we will turn the international spotlight away from an area of the world that still needs it. Worse, we will stop listening for the cries of girls who are exploited.

Now we were both angered. My human nature wants me to spend time convincing you I was right, but that's not the point. The point is we were two partners that had honored and served each other for years in the midst of an ugly conflict, but we had failed to communicate with each other.

I should have prepared our partner for the CNN documentary. They should have communicated with us before sending the op-ed piece. I should have communicated with them before sending my op-ed piece. If we had communicated with one another we could have jointly communicated in a way that celebrated the progress made without discounting there was still a long ways to go. I believe we could have done that. Instead, we presented a public face of enmity.

A few months later our partner's leadership team and ours met in Svay Pak. We reconciled our differences; however, sadly our partnership never regained the intimacy and mutual support we once had. I pray we never again let this happen.

## YOU'RE OUTTA HERE!

In late July 2017, CNN aired an update to *Every Day in Cambodia*. This documentary followed up with the girls from the first piece in 2015 and added interviews with their mothers who were involved in their trafficking. The headline on the CNN website read, "Cambodian Mothers Sell Their Daughters."

Initially, things were quiet, but that didn't last. A leader of a Cambodian journalist group wrote a letter to the Cambodian prime minister saying AIM was disparaging Cambodian mothers and never used donations made to help the Cambodian people. It claimed Don Brewster and his wife were getting rich instead of helping people.

Upon receipt of that letter the prime minister went on national television and announced he was kicking AIM out of Cambodia, effective immediately! The announcement was picked up by international news outlets like CNN and *The Guardian*. Donations dropped. I was called to meet with the Cambodian police.

Over a ten-day period I spent long hours being questioned by the Cambodian police and a number of Cambodian government leaders. I was only able to catch a couple hours of sleep as evenings were spent preparing documents to answer questions I couldn't fully answer during the meetings. Truth is, I had it easy compared to Bridget.

Bridget had to handle the swarm of news agencies that flooded Svay Pak and calm the nerves of our staff who were sure this was the end of AIM. It was understandable they felt this way: a number of organizations had been shut down by the Cambodian government, and there were none who had survived once the prime minister said they were out.

Bridget got our staff praying along with hundreds of AIM supporters around the globe. The news agencies coming to Svay Pak interviewed dozens of residents and every one of them was supportive of AIM, not wanting us gone. It was a stark difference from the early days when we were getting death threats. God was answering our prayers.

The meetings with the police and government leaders ended with them being supportive of our staying in Cambodia, but the decision was Prime Minister Hun Sen's. They suggested I write a letter of apology to the prime minister. Here is what I sent . . .

> *8 August 2017*
>
> *To: His Excellency Samedach Hun Sen–Prime Minister of Cambodia and to all Cambodia*
>
> *From: Dr. Don Brewster–Chief Executive Officer–Agape International Mission (AIM)*
>
> I would like to express my great love and respect for the Kingdom of Cambodia and the Cambodian people. This is reflected in my decision to leave my 4 children and 12 grandchildren in America to serve the Cambodian people. I would also like to express my deep sorrow for any hurt or harm inflicted on Cambodia and her people that resulted from the CNN Freedom Project broadcast.
>
> CNN contacted me and asked to interview three girls from Svay Pak they had interviewed in the past after their rescue from sex trafficking. The purpose was to show the new good life they now shared in Svay Pak. I told CNN that it was the girls' decision and then asked

## Chapter 13: Conflict

the girls if they wanted to be interviewed. All the girls said yes because they wanted to help other victims of sex trafficking to have hope that they too can have a good life. They also wished to bring awareness to the sex trafficking happening all around the world. I also believed their sharing would give hope to victims and show the significant improvements made in Svay Pak and all of Cambodia through the Cambodian government's efforts.

Unfortunately, CNN identified the three girls as Cambodian when in fact they are ethnically Vietnamese. This misidentification was made even though I told CNN the girls were Vietnamese. It is clear this was the case as CNN spoke to the girls in the Vietnamese language. I have written CNN to point out this error and they did correct their website. In addition, I am happy to write them again; however, it should be noted I have no authority or influence with CNN over what they say or do.

AIM was incorporated in 1988 in America and initially served as a church planting NGO in Cambodia. I was the chairman of the board of directors and supervisor. Dr. Moses Samol Seth was the executive director in Cambodia. In 2005, the mission of AIM changed to fight against sex trafficking in Cambodia and around the world. At that time AIM registered as an international NGO with the Ministry of Foreign Affairs, I became the executive director, and Dr. Seth registered the church planting program as a local NGO with the Ministry of Interior.

Since 2005 AIM has initiated 14 different programs in Cambodia which have helped more than 130,000 Cambodians. None of these people would have been helped without the cooperation and efforts of the Cambodian government and people. We are grateful and honored to work with the Cambodian government. The purpose of these 14 programs is to prevent sex trafficking, rescue victims of sex trafficking, bring restoration to the rescued victims, and reintegrate the restored former victims as productive young women with self-sustaining employment. The 14 programs are as follows.

**Agape Restoration Center**–Provided aftercare for 400 rescued victims of sex trafficking.

**Rahab's House Phnom Penh**–Provided aftercare for 126 victims of sex trafficking.

**Emergency Foster Care**–Prevented the trafficking of 62 at-risk children.

**Rahab's House School**–Prevents the trafficking of children by providing high-quality education. 1,189 children have been helped. We are in the process of constructing a new school for 1,500 students.

***Lord's Gym**-Prevents trafficking through traditional Khmer boxing combined with mentoring and life skills training. Helped 185 young men, including 2 national champions.

**Agape Training Center 1**-Provides vocational and life skills training to former victims being reintegrated back into Cambodian society. Also, prevents re-trafficking. 147 young women helped.

**Agape Training Center 2**-Prevents trafficking by providing vocational and life skills training to at-risk young women and men. Helped 575.

**Agape Training Center 3**-Provides vocational and life skills training to former victims being reintegrated back into Cambodian society. Also, prevents re-trafficking. 20 young women helped.

**Rahab's House Siem Reap**-Provided aftercare for 126 rescued victims of sex trafficking.

**Rahab's House Lotus Kids' Club**-Prevents trafficking of at-risk children by providing preschool education and support for attending primary school. 143 children helped.

**Rahab's House Church**-Prevents sex trafficking by providing moral, life skills, and community health education. 352 families helped.

**Mentoring/Discipleship Program**-Prevents trafficking by providing a 3-year program which supports the completion of the last 3 years of high school with room and board, tutoring, life skills, and moral training. In addition, supports those who qualify to attend university. 278 students helped.

**Humanitarian Aid and Disaster Relief**-Prevents trafficking by providing material help ranging from food and medical help to repairing houses. Helped 127,416 families and individuals.

**AIM SWAT**-Rescues victims by assisting the AHTJP with cases of human trafficking. Helped with 80 cases resulting in 142 arrests and 429 rescues.*

The 2017 budget for these 14 programs is 2,965,212 USD. This does not include the construction budgets in excess of 1,500,00 USD. Details for each program can be found in the attached report, as well as the Memorandums of Understanding with the Ministry of Foreign Affairs, Ministry of Education, Ministry of Social Affairs, Ministry of Religion and Cults, and the Anti-Human Trafficking and Juvenile Protection Police. Also please see attachments for further details including letters of gratitude and attestation for the Ministry of Foreign Affairs and AHTJP, and the highest award available in America for integrity in the collection and use of funds provided by donors awarded to AIM.

## Chapter 13: Conflict

> *In closing I want to restate my and AIM's commitment to the people and government of Cambodia to always act in a way which always reflects our love and respect for both. And once again, although I have no authority or influence with CNN, I will gladly write to them again.*
>
> Sincerely,
> Don Brewster - CEO Agape International Missions
> CC:  Ministry of Interior
> Ministry of Foreign Affairs
> Ministry of Education
> Ministry of Social Affairs
> Anti-Human Trafficking and Juvenile Protection Police
> Attachments:
> AIM Program Details
> Memorandums of Understanding
> Letter of Achievement from AHTJP
> Letter of Gratitude from the Ministry of Foreign Affairs
> Letter of Attestation from the AHTJP
> Award for Highest Integrity in collection
>   and Use of Donations
> AIM Organizational Chart

After I sent the letter, our staff and supporters waited anxiously for the prime minister's response. He asked that I call for a press conference in which I would read the letter I sent him, followed by time for those assembled to ask questions. His answer about our future would come later. I was cool with reading the letter, and not too concerned about the questions. However, our staff person selected to translated for me was not cool. The poor guy was sweating bullets. He was committed to translating me accurately, was confident about the letter reading, but very nervous about the Q & A. I needed to be careful not to use American idioms or English words that would be difficult to translate.

The room was packed with journalists from a wide assortment of media, print, radio, TV, and podcasts. The initial questions came from the man who had written the accusatory letter to the prime minister. They weren't really questions, they were baseless accusations. After a few minutes, I told him he could no longer ask questions. The rest of the questioning, almost one hour, primarily focused on what I thought of the Cambodian government. I was happy to say I was grateful the government gave me the opportunity to respond to accusations.

Now we waited to hear the prime minister's decision. It came in an unexpected way. Once again on Cambodian national television, Prime Minster Hun Sen announced AIM could stay. A short time later he presented me with a medal to honor the substantial work AIM had done to benefit the country of Cambodia. What an unbelievable turnaround!

## RESPONDING TO THE UNEXPECTED

It would be easy to think of this monumental turnaround as the logical conclusion of AIM's history of doing good in Jesus' name. However, the logical conclusion, backed by history, is when the prime minister says, "You're out!," you're out. I have no doubt the surprising conclusion was the result of immediately turning to God, prayer, and his grace. In this case our immediately turning to God was not based on spiritual maturity, it was the result of our hopelessness. In the future it would be best to turn to God when the unexpected seems easy to overcome, or is a good thing. Regardless of the circumstance the best place to start is with God.

And better yet, when it comes to those we share life with, do all we can to minimize the unexpected.

# CHAPTER 14: WHY?

## WHY CARE ABOUT SEX TRAFFICKING IN OTHER COUNTRIES?

THAT'S A GREAT QUESTION. Why should we care? After all, there's plenty of sex trafficking going on right here in the United States. Why concern ourselves about what is happening around the globe when we have our own issues? Actually, there are many good reasons, but I'm going to focus on just four. These four reasons can apply to any other country; however, they are most evident in our relationship with developing countries because of our position as one of the richest, most powerful nations in the world. To illustrate these reasons I'm choosing to use Cambodia. This, of course, should be no surprise as our ministry, AIM, has been fighting sex trafficking there for nearly two decades.

## Reason #1–God Commands Us

*Then Jesus came to them and said, "All authority in heaven and on earth has been given to me. Therefore go and make disciples of **all nations**, baptizing them in the name of the Father and of the Son and of the Holy Spirit, and teaching them to obey everything I have commanded you. And surely I am with you always, to the very end of the age" (Matt 28:18-20 NIV).*

Wow, don't you feel like this should be a "mic drop" moment and we all just go do something? We could, but God gives us more to consider. For example, throughout the Bible God calls us to stand with the oppressed and fight injustice. *"Learn to do right; seek justice. Defend the oppressed. Take up the cause of the fatherless; plead the case of the widow" (Isa 1:17 NIV).* And in 2 Corinthians 8 and 9, those who are rich in resources are told to share them with those with less.

It seems clear. God's commandments to us should be enough, right? Still, we'll continue with reasons two, three, and four as they help us see the "why" of God's commandments.

## Reason #2–We Are Part of the Problem

When there is a problem like the evil of child sex trafficking in another country it's easy to focus on what's wrong with them and be blinded to the part we have played and are playing. In some places, the connection is quite subtle; however, that's not the case in Cambodia.

During the Vietnam War, Cambodia was caught in the middle of fierce fighting. Even though the nation was a US ally, Cambodia sadly became collateral damage in the effort to stop the spread of communism in Southeast Asia. At the end of the war, the United States military withdrew from Cambodia and left little economic or military support. The disruption in Cambodia caused by the Vietnam War opened up the door to the Khmer Rouge, carrying out one of the most destructive genocides in history. This, and the resulting poverty, played a significant role in the spread of sex trafficking in Cambodia.

Today we continue to be a part of the problem. American sex tourists and pedophiles still visit Cambodia to sexually abuse and exploit both women and children. It's not just the nation that's part of the problem, it extends to the church as well. How? The use of porn.

Recent research by the Barna Group reveals porn use is a pandemic in our churches. We are no different from the world when it comes to consuming porn. That's alarming! Just as alarming is the fact that we don't truly understand the devastation caused by porn to the users, their families, their church, and our culture! If that wasn't enough, our use of porn fuels sex trafficking and the abuse and exploitation of women and children around the globe.

Read "Overcoming the Porn Pandemic in the Church," found in Appendix 3, to better understand the problem and how each of us can help.

## Reason #3–We Are God's Solution

The world thinks evil is defeated through education, economic development, and legal justice. These are good things and they are all a part of our ministry in Cambodia. However, world history, including American

## Chapter 14: Why?

history, shows those efforts do not defeat evil. In fact, they're often used for evil. Instead, defeating evil—and revealing the healing and transformation of those hurt by evil—is found only in Jesus' love.

It is a slow process, one life at a time. But, when we persevere in Jesus' love we see the transformation of an individual, then a family, and then a community and beyond. We know this is true because the Bible tells us so. Simply put, Jesus defeated evil on the cross. In addition, we have experienced this to be true as caring American churches have supported our efforts to be conduits of his love.

So, yes, American Christians should care about sex trafficking in other countries. AIM is grateful to partner with local congregations across the United States who are stepping up to the plate in order to combat sex trafficking by proclaiming hope in the name of Jesus.

I hope you'll take some time to experience this truth by watching a documentary that shares the story of a young Cambodian girl who went from being a horribly abused victim of an American pedophile to becoming a courageous modern-day abolitionist. You can see it at https://vimeo.com/545323935/75bdc5636b.

### Reason #4–We're Blessed

The obedience Jesus requires of us is motivated by our love for him. With this loving obedience we experience his love for, and pleasure with, us. We experience joy! Jesus speaks to this truth in John 15:9-13 NLT.

> I have loved you even as the Father has loved me. Remain in my love. When you obey my commandments, you remain in my love, just as I obey my Father's commandments and remain in his love. I have told you these things so that you will be filled with my joy. Yes, your joy will overflow! This is my commandment: Love each other in the same way I have loved you. There is no greater love than to lay down one's life for one's friends.

### NOT LOOKING AWAY

As you probably already guessed, the overwhelming evil I would like you not to look away from is child sex trafficking. As I noted before, joining the fight against child sex trafficking will result in some people leaving their homes like Bridget and I did. Some will open their homes for a vulnerable child. (In the US most of the rescued child victims of sex trafficking come from the foster care system.) Some will change the way they live in their homes. (They'll buy ethically produced products and join the fight against pornography.) There are literally dozens of ways to get involved. You can check them out on our website, www.aimfree.org. However, it's important to remember not to over-complicate this. Simply put, we use what God has given us in a way that fights evil. We have many examples of how this works, but the coolest example is in Hong Kong.

## The Hong Kong Example

I still can't get over how God used one man's God-given gift to enlist so many to use theirs to fight child sex trafficking in Cambodia. It all started with Benji Nolet.

*Benji Nolet*

Benji's gift is making films. When he heard about the evil of sex trafficking he used his gift to create a documentary film, *Nefarious: Merchant of Souls* to build awareness of the issue. (You can see the film on YouTube.) The work of AIM was highlighted in the film. The following is one of many impacts the film made around the world. Please note the names of the people in Hong Kong have been changed due to the current relationship between China and the United States.

*Melinda*

Melinda watched the film and knew she had to do something. She wasn't wealthy. She could give a little and pray, but wanted to do more. Her time was limited as she was suffering from stage four cancer. So she decided to show the film to her Bible study group and anyone else she could. Many of the people who saw it were moved to act.

*Jerry*

Jerry was a sixteen-year-old gifted artist. He painted a picture of a young Cambodian boy and sold it, with the proceeds donated to AIM.

# Chapter 14: Why?

*Martha*

Martha was involved with the youth group in her church and led a team of kids from the group to aid in a construction project in Svay Pak.

*Richard*

Richard was a businessman who owned a garment factory in Cambodia. He outfitted a small facility in Svay Pak to provide good jobs to our girls for a couple of years while we were building up our employment center.

*Lisa*

Lisa was involved in her church's missions ministry. She introduced AIM to the church and lobbied to give me an opportunity to speak at Sunday services. I was given several opportunities and over a couple of years the church donated over one million US dollars to AIM. We'll return to Lisa after George.

*George*

George worked in the finance world. He used his connections to host a fundraiser, with all of the donations going to AIM.

*Lisa*

(I have already shared this part of her story in chapter 7, but it is worth repeating in context.) Cambodian girls were being trafficked to mainland China, but since we did not work there they were beyond our reach. One of these girls, Gracie, escaped, and while on the run miraculously was given our phone number. (That's a long story for another book.) She called, told us her story, and asked for help getting home. At that moment we didn't know how to help. She had a cell phone so we could call her back.

Immediately, we met with the Cambodian government and were told to have her go to the Cambodian embassy in Beijing and she would get help. We gave her the news and felt good it was so easy to help. Only it wasn't so easy. When she got to the building that housed the embassy and a number of other organization's offices the security guards wouldn't let her in.

Gracie called us again and explained her new problem. We told her to stay where she was and we would call her back. More attempts to get her in the building failed. We were running out of options. It was then I remembered Lisa had connections in Beijing. I called her to ask if she knew someone who could help. She said she was in Beijing and wanted to know how she could help.

I explained the problem and asked if she could help. She agreed to go get Gracie. She wasn't sure her husband would agree, so she kind of snuck out of the hotel where they were staying. Again we began congratulating ourselves on a problem solved. Once again it was premature. When Lisa got to the embassy building Gracie refused to go with her. Immediately we called Gracie and explained Lisa was there to help her, and to please go with her now.

Finally things were looking up. Then Lisa called to say the security guards were now trying to stop Gracie from getting in the car with her. I responded, "Lisa, you're going to need to man up. Throw Gracie in your car and take off!" She said, "Really?" I said, "Yes!" and hung up. Later I realized it was very unlikely Lisa understood my idiom "man up."

Within a few minutes Lisa called and joyously announced, "I got her!," immediately following up with, "Now what do I do with her?" That was a good question—we hadn't gotten that far. Thankfully it didn't take long for me to remember one of the businessmen who attended the fundraiser. He managed a beautiful property and he provided a safe place for Gracie to stay until we could work out the details to get her home.

While Gracie waited she called others Cambodian girls who were living as trafficking victims in China. Her sharing our number led to sixty-one more rescues. It's amazing what God can do when we don't look away.

One more thing about Lisa and Gracie... Lisa has come to Cambodia to visit Gracie and has helped start her own small business.

There's actually significantly more people who used their gifts, but you get the idea.

## WHERE TO LOOK

While your involvement in the fight against sex trafficking would be awesome, there are a number of overwhelming evils God may call you to fight.

## Chapter 14: Why?

My prayer is you would hear clearly, and step out in faith. As our experience reveals God can bring transformation when we say "yes" to his call; miracles happen when we do. Jesus has promised us this:

> I tell you the truth, anyone who believes in me will do the same works I have done, and even greater works, because I am going to be with the Father. (John 14:12 NLT)

The "you" in this verse is a plural pronoun, indicating our unity in acting will bring about the greater works. If we consider the great works accomplished by Christians throughout the years it seems they are always started by one stepping out in faith. Maybe it will be you.

DON'T LOOK AWAY
SAY YES TO THE ONE
The one Lord Jesus Christ, and the one in need standing before you.
"Don't let evil conquer you, but conquer evil by doing good" (Rom 12:21 NLT).

# ACKNOWLEDGMENTS

I'D LIKE TO BEGIN by thanking Kevin Holst for his encouragement to write this book, and his introduction to Mark Beuving who believed in the book, and shared his expertise without which it would not have been written.

Mira Sorvino is a committed abolitionist who has used her platform to impact women and children around the world. Thank you for your support and encouragement, and writing the foreword to this book.

Longtime supporter Gene Krcelic volunteered his experience, gifts, and talents to help edit this book. The result of his hours of effort is a far, far better book.

The AIM board of directors and Bridget Brewster never wavered in their support and encouragement through the long process of writing and publishing this book, a much longer process than anyone anticipated.

Finally, the content of this book is the result of AIM staff, volunteers, and supporters who chose not to look away, but instead, say yes to the one. I am forever in your debt.

# APPENDIX 1

## Sophia's Story

MY NAME IS SOPHIA. I have chosen to share my story so that it may bring help and inspiration to girls who have suffered in the same way I have. Also, I hope it will help others to protect themselves from the evil and pain of sex trafficking.

When I was twelve years old my mother sold me to a foreign man, an American. When I was rescued I was sent to a transitional center to prepare me to move into an aftercare home. People were nice there, but I knew I wouldn't be staying there. After a few weeks I visited several aftercare homes and was given the opportunity to choose the one where I would go. I chose to go to ARH (Agape Restoration Home). There were several reasons I chose ARH. When I visited the social workers explained to me all the opportunities I would have there, the most important of which was getting a good education. I believed them. I believed them because I sensed that they really cared about me.

I wasn't disappointed! There was comfort staying there and the promise of a good education was fulfilled; however, more importantly I felt loved. I felt compassion. I felt encouraged and it gave me hope. ARH also gave me a family. It was like being born again. There were rules and a daily structure, rights and responsibilities, and they taught me right from wrong. Not only in words, but by their example too. The staff loved me when I did right, and when I did wrong! They loved me even though I could do nothing to benefit them.

If I was sad, crying, or just having a bad day my social worker or counselor always made time to comfort me no matter how busy she was. This

## Appendix 1

is my best memory. My favorite thing to do was to go to school and study, except for art. But I did like learning Apsara dancing.

When I came to ARH I didn't believe in Jesus, and I only kind of believed in him when I left ARH for the first time. You see, I had two different stays at ARH. At the end of my first stay I chose to be reintegrated before the staff thought I was ready, but I felt sure I was ready. I could now read and write, and on a home visit with my mom and aunt they convinced me things would be different.

At first things were different than before, but that didn't last very long. I soon felt like a failure because I couldn't protect myself from my mom and aunt's abuse. It became perfectly clear leaving ARH was a mistake when they sold me to a brothel. I did not want to go, but I had no choice as my aunt had already taken the money.

Once I got to the brothel I pleaded with the pimp to let me go. His response was always the same, "No! Your aunt still owes me money." After many months, more than a year, I got pregnant. I didn't realize this for the first three months of pregnancy; after that it became obvious. I asked the pimp to leave again, but again he said, "No! Your aunt still owes me money." He also told me I had to get an abortion and go back to work until the debt was paid in full. I decided to call my mom and aunt for advice. They told me to have the abortion and go back to work. So I got the abortion. I was left alone at the clinic and even though I was in great pain I ran away. I went back home.

After being home only two months my aunt began selling me to foreign men from many different countries. I was just thirteen years old. I was forced to stay two days with each man. During this time I got a phone and called my ARH social worker. This led to my second rescue and my second stay at ARH.

Coming back to ARH was like getting my life back, although I was embarrassed at first to see the staff and other girls. I was worried about what they would think of me, having to come back a second time. My concerns melted away at my princess party where I felt welcomed, valued, and loved! *(Note: At ARH we have a princess party for each rescued girl as she enters our aftercare home. Among other things she receives a princess crown as a symbol of her royalty as a child of God.)*

My second stay at ARH was like the first one. Counseling, school, and being loved and cared for like before, maybe even more. The additional time made a big difference. I attended an English school, received vocational training, and started a job prior to leaving ARH. I was so happy! In preparation for my leaving I received additional education in managing my money and budgeting.

My reintegration was very different too. Instead of going back to my mom and aunt I was reintegrated with a couple other ARH girls. Our social workers helped us find a nice room to rent, and I bought a bike to ride back and forth to work. My life was very good. I had a good job, at a good place, with people who cared about me. Then I met a guy who I thought was a good one, but he wasn't. I learned he was a drug dealer and gang member. When I tried to break off our relationship he became violent and abusive. I needed protection. When I met with my ARH social worker she helped me relocate to another town.

Once there I decided to continue my education while working full time. The job skills I had made it easy to find a new job, but I wanted to learn more. Once again, things were going well when a family problem came into my life. I felt so depressed, I was certain there was no hope for me to have a good life. Sad and dejected, I moved to another town. My social worker continued to meet with me and helped me move to Phnom Penh and find a job at AIM's Employment Center.

While I didn't have the skill to do the job, AIM's Employment Center provided the training. This place is more than a place to work, it is a place where a girl is loved and valued. It is also the place where I found the man I love, a man who became my husband. After working there a little less than a year I was offered a job on the newly formed AIM SWAT Team. It was a job where I could use my education and life experience to help rescue girls and help those who were rescued. I was told to take my time in deciding, but I didn't need the time. I knew this was something I wanted to do, to help others as I had been helped. So I immediately said, "Yes!"

Since saying yes a lot has happened. I have helped rescue and care for hundreds of victims of sex trafficking. I am happily married to the guy I met at the employment center and we have two beautiful daughters. I have fully put my faith in Jesus. When times of doubt enter my mind I remember how greatly he has blessed me through the Christians he brought into my life. I have forgiven my mom. She stays in a room next door to me and my family. We have dinner together most nights. Sometimes it gets uncomfortable, but I am committed to be a light of Jesus in her life.

# Appendix 1

Today my family is much larger than those living in my home, it's the family of God. To this very day I stay in touch with that part of my family at ARH.

*Eric Meldrum, the director of AIM SWAT, has this to say about Sophia:*

*"Sophia is an exceptional member of the SWAT team and brings unique qualities that enable her to undertake investigative tasks that no one else can do. She's a survivor from a terrible situation as a child, but those qualities that enabled her to survive make her such an asset—incredibly strong, brave, quick thinking, and now motivated to help girls who are suffering and bring their traffickers to justice. From the darkness she experienced she is now bringing light and actively combatting the evil of child sex trafficking. If that wasn't enough she's also a great mom to her two girls. We simply couldn't do without her on the SWAT team."*

# APPENDIX 2

# Linda's Story

When I was rescued my mother was arrested and sent to prison for trafficking me and some other girls as well. As I walked into ARH (Agape Restoration Home) I felt happy, joyful, and free. I saw the swimming pool and I was very happy. It was the beginning of a new life for me. There were people who loved and cared for me. It was the first time I felt this kind of love. I was loved simply because I was there.

I also loved going to school. I had the opportunity to study and be whatever I wanted. In the past I would only go to school for a month or so, then my mom would pull me out. ARH gave me freedom, but to be honest I didn't get as much freedom as I wanted. I wanted to do whatever I wanted, whenever I wanted.

The only times I felt deep sorrow was when I visited my mom in prison. ARH staff would take me every month. I would bring her food and soap. My sorrow was deepened because my little brother was in prison with my mom. I would beg her to let ARH find an organization to take care of him while she was in prison, but she didn't want that. *(Note: In Cambodia mothers sentenced to prison can bring their young children to prison with them. These are co-ed prisons which include violent criminals. Some mothers choose to do this because they are offered additional support from organizations that help prisoners, while others feel they have no other choice.)* The reason my brother went to live with my mom in prison was that my sister and I were too young and in the care of different organizations. My brother was younger and left without care. Our stepdad, who's my brother's biological father, went to live with another women after my mom was in prison just four months. He left with no one to watch my brother so it was decided that my brother would go and live with my mom.

At ARH I chose to believe in Jesus, but it didn't happen at first. One day my house mom gave us girls the challenge, to memorize 1 Corinthians 13. I am very competitive and I wanted to be the first girl to memorize it. I worked very hard and one day I stood up in devotions and recited it perfectly in front of the staff and all the girls. I won the challenge, but I didn't really believe the words. Over time that changed.

Every day I would see the staff and the way they lived. They were very different from the people I knew in my past. They lived a life of love. Because of their example I began to believe in Jesus. Then I studied the words of 1 Corinthians 13. I believed them, and they changed me.

Eventually, I was reintegrated to live with my older sister and aunt. I was a little worried that now I would be doing everything for myself, but I was very happy to be with my family, especially because my mom let my little brother leave the prison and he was living with us.

I started working at a bakery and it was pretty good. My ARH social worker continued to meet with me and provide encouragement. Actually my social worker continues to follow up with me even as an adult. She is always encouraging and reminds me of my forever family at ARH.

When I would come home from work I would see so many poor children in my neighborhood who didn't have the opportunity to go to school and get an education. Jesus put it on my heart to share what I learned at ARH, so I started a tiny little school. Every day after work I would teach lessons. When my social worker found out what I was doing she asked ARH to help by getting books and school supplies.

In the meantime things were going so well at work. My boss saw I could design and create beautiful things out of sugar. Soon I was promoted to training others, and not long after that I was promoted to department manager.

After working for three years at the bakery I met a man who would become my husband. He, like me, is a Christian. On our first date we went to church together. Soon we were married. After a couple of years God blessed us with a beautiful baby girl.

I continued to work at the bakery. One day they decided to open a second location and they sent me to do the training. Later, they opened a third location and I was promoted to be the manager. I worked at that bakery for ten years. A year ago I decided to take all my experience to start my

## Appendix 2

own business selling food and clothes. It has been a little difficult because of COVID, but I am excited about what the future holds for me and my family.

I don't forget about my past, but I don't let it control me. I have forgiven those who hurt me. I am happy to share my story to help the girls and women of Cambodia. I have even traveled to a foreign country to share it. Jesus is most important to me. He comforts me in times of trouble. He transformed my life.

# APPENDIX 3

## Overcoming the Porn Pandemic in the Church

Don Brewster, Agape International Missions
September 2021

### INTRODUCTION

Now doesn't seem to be the best time to be addressing a very heavy subject. After all we are in the midst of a COVID pandemic, and our country is experiencing an unheard-of level of divisiveness. Together they are wreaking havoc on American families. At the same time there is a silent pandemic not only hurting our families, but resulting in the abuse of women and children around the globe. This pandemic is running rampant through the church and most churches are not addressing it.

We Christians are fueling sex trafficking and the rape of women and children around the globe. How? By using porn. Sound hyperbolic? It's not, it's a fact. And I have seen firsthand the result of our porn use.

Fifteen years ago I left my position as the executive pastor of a church in California and moved with my wife, Bridget, to Cambodia, where we founded an anti-trafficking ministry, Agape International Missions (AIM). The ministry *rescues* child victims of sex trafficking, provides *restoration* homes for their healing, then empowers them for *reintegration* back into society as productive and capable young women. We have seen in the faces of hundreds of rescued victims the pain, fear, shame, and guilt resulting from their abuse. By God's grace and through his love we have witnessed hundreds of successful restorations and reintegrations. Truly good things, miraculous stuff, but not the stuff that will reduce the number of women and children being sex trafficked in the future.

## APPENDIX 3

What became clear was the need for an effective means of preventing sex trafficking. Prevention falls into two categories: protecting the vulnerable and reducing demand. For example, in the US, protecting the vulnerable includes becoming foster parents or a Court Appointed Special Advocate (CASA) for a foster child. However, the most effective means of prevention is reducing demand. Laws and their enforcement, education, and economic development can help reduce demand, but they're not enough. They don't defeat evil. *As long as men are willing to buy women and children, evil will devise the means to deliver them.* I've often jokingly said, "The most effective way to end the trafficking and abuse is to execute all men. Being one of them I'm not in favor of this method." There is means of reducing demand I can support—reducing the use of porn. Below we'll take a look at how using porn fuels sex trafficking and the abuse of women and children globally, as well as some of the other harm it causes. Then we'll examine the pandemic of porn in the church and what we can do to eliminate it. The harm of porn and the extent of its use is hard to hear, but by using the tools God has given us to overcome it, the church has an opportunity to make a global impact in protecting women and children without leaving home.

## THE PREVALENCE AND IMPACT OF PORN

Simply put, porn is ubiquitous—it's everywhere. It's easy to see how the sexualization of our society has brought sexual explicit images to primetime television, even its advertisements, not to mention the no-holds-barred content on Netflix, Amazon Prime, and other paid streaming services available on multiple devices.

Porn and the methods for accessing it have evolved. Today's porn has few legal restraints, and combined with the sexualization of our culture results in it becoming more hard core, dehumanizing, and abusive. In the past, using porn took some effort on the part of users. Today it pops up on our phones, tablets, and computers, even when we're not looking for it, tempting us while at the same time keeping our use of it hidden from others.

The sexualization of our culture has resulted in pornography becoming normalized and entering the cultural mainstream. Pornography has also become more explicit, violent, and racist.

The definition of porn can be argued. For our purposes, we will narrow porn to content that includes images of sexual acts, used for sexual arousal, and found on the internet.

APPENDIX 3

## Let's look at some facts . . .

The porn industry is massive in scope and destruction. *Porn revenue* is difficult to track due to its makers and distributors being privately held. That said, researchers found worldwide pornography revenues from a variety of sources (the internet, sex shops, videos rented in hotel rooms) were approximately *$100 billion in 2010*.[1] That staggering amount of money is *more than the combined revenues of Microsoft, Google, Amazon, eBay, Yahoo, Apple, and Netflix that same year.*[2]

By being online, this places the most violent and sadistic sexual abuse on the phones in our children's pockets, just a pop-up and click away. Ninety-five percent of teens report they have a smartphone or access to one.[3] Forty-five percent of teens say they are online on a constant basis.[4]

The porn industry has moved almost completely to being an online product with almost all of the content being bought off contractors and no longer being made by the sites themselves.[5] Ninety percent of free porn websites and nearly 100 percent of pay porn websites buy their material rather than create it themselves.[6]

The use of contractors means anyone with a smartphone can produce and upload porn, thus minimizing the liability and expenses of the websites distributing the porn. At the same time, it increases the use of rape and trafficking victims by producers, while their anonymity reduces their risk of being caught.

The question then becomes: how much porn is out there and how often is it viewed? Consider the facts: Google, the most used search engine in the world, revealed on its list of most-searched sites that PornHub, one of the most popular porn websites, ranks number four, just behind Facebook, YouTube, and Amazon.[7]

1. Jerry Ropelato, "Internet Pornography Statistics," table 2. https://ministryoftruth.me.uk/wp-content/uploads/2014/03/IFR2013.pdf.

2. Jerry Ropelato, "Internet Pornography Statistics," para. 3.

3. Pew Research Center, "Teens, Social Media and Technology 2018," para. 2. https://www.pewresearch.org/internet/2018/05/31/teens-social-media-technology-2018/.

4. Pew Research Center, "Teens, Social Media and Technology 2018," para. 2.

5. Matthew Zook, "Report on the location of the Internet adult industry," in *C'Lick Me: A Netporn Studies Reader*, ed. Katrien Jacobs, Marije Janssen, and Matteo Pasquinelli (Amsterdam: Institute of Network Cultures, 2007), 103–21. http://www.networkcultures.org/_uploads/24.pdf.

6. Zook, "Report on the location of the Internet adult industry," 104.

7. https://docs.google.com/spreadsheets/d/1mlHF56hFspD7FNfQQ2qOO7LPCqJ72

APPENDIX 3

| Keyword | Search Volume |
|---|---|
| Facebook | 151,500,000 |
| YouTube | 142,200,000 |
| Amazon | 87,440,000 |
| PornHub | 86,250,000 |

Google "Most Searched USA 2020 (Accessed May 26, 2020)[8]

PornHub ranks higher than the combined totals of Netflix, Fox New, CNN, and Instagram.[9]

The internet is used at least 13 percent of the time for viewing adult content on the over 42,000 porn sites in existence, and that number is growing daily.[10]

| PornHub | 2017 | 2019 |
|---|---|---|
| Annual Website Visits | 28.5 billion | 42 billion |
| Daily Average Visits | 81 million | 115 million |
| Website Searches | 25 billion | 39 billion |
| Uploaded Videos | 4.05 million | 6.83 million |
| Years of Content Uploaded | 68 years | 169 years |

*The size and growth of porn is reflected in PornHub's numbers.*[11]

Taking a minute to analyze those numbers reveals some sad but important truths.

vQdL2wk4pYcTCs/copy.

8. https://docs.google.com/spreadsheets/d/1mlHF56hFspD7FNfQQ2qOO7LPCqJ7 2vQdL2wk4pYcTCs/copy.

9. Ibi https://docs.google.com/spreadsheets/d/1mlHF56hFspD7FNfQQ2qOO7LPCq J72vQdL2wk4pYcTCs/copy.

10. Julie Ruvolo, "How Much of the Internet is Actually Porn," para. 7. https://www.forbes.com/sites/julieruvolo/2011/09/07/how-much-of-the-internet-is-actually-for-porn/#158dabb45d16.

11. Fight the New Drug, "The Most Viewed Porn Categories Of 2017 Are Pretty Messed Up," table 1, https://fightthenewdrug.org/pornhub-reports-most-viewed-porn-of-2017/, and "Pornhub's Annual Report: Can You Guess the Most Popular Porn Categories in 2019?," table 1, https://fightthenewdrug.org/2019-pornhub-annual-report/.

The two-year growth rate in PornHub visits is over 40 percent. Demand for porn is growing exponentially.

This is further supported as the numbers indicate as many as 93 percent of people landing on the website search for more content. Even if people are landing there accidentally, once they arrive, they look around.

Independent contractors have increased the number of videos they upload by 68 percent, making for 169 years of content, or 88,826,400 minutes.

If PornHub were to vet that content by merely watching the videos, it would take a team of twenty full-time staff over forty-five years to accomplish the task. Of course this is not done, and the result is horrific content.

An investigation into PornHub reported finding "dozens" of illegal abuse videos within "minutes," including abuse images of children as young as three years old. Some of the videos identified by the investigation "had 350,000 views and had been on the platform for more than three years. Three of the worst clips still remained on the site 24 hours later."[12]

We must not forget PornHub is just one of over 42,000 porn websites.

## So who's watching porn and what's their attitude about it?

Research shows that a range of 51 to 64 percent of Americans use porn at least occasionally. What's not surprising is the older you are, the more likely you'll consider porn bad and are likely not to be forthcoming about your use of it. Thus these reported numbers are likely lower than the reality.

Let's take a look at the numbers.

> 51 percent of all Americans use porn at least occasionally[13]
> 46 percent of all American males use porn regularly[14]
> 47 percent of all American males twenty-five plus use porn regularly[15]
> 67 percent of all American males thirteen to twenty-four use porn regularly[16]
> 18 percent of all American females use porn regularly[17]

12. Traffickinghub, https://traffickinghub.com/.
13. McDowell/Barna, "The Porn Phenomenon," 37.
14. McDowell/Barna, "The Porn Phenomenon," 42.
15. McDowell/Barna, "The Porn Phenomenon," 32.
16. McDowell/Barna, "The Porn Phenomenon," 32.
17. Luke Gilkerson, "How Many Women are Hooked on Porn? 10 Stats that May Shock You," list 1, number 5. https://www.covenanteyes.com/2013/08/30/

## APPENDIX 3

12 percent of all American females twenty-five plus use porn regularly[18]

33 percent of all American females thirteen to twenty-four use porn regularly[19]

Among all ages of adults in the United States, 64 percent of men and 42 percent of women view pornography at least monthly.[20]

After the internet made pornography readily available in the first decade of the twenty-first century, research showed that 86 percent of men were viewing pornography.[21, 22]

Again, these numbers are alarming in what they reveal, even more so when we consider older Americans, especially Christians, are likely to consider porn use wrong or embarrassing and underreport its use. With that in mind the numbers still reveal:

- That most Americans use porn.
- The younger you are (and most susceptible to the damage caused by porn), the more likely you are to use it.
- Where porn used to be considered a male issue, we now see it as a significant and growing issue for both genders.

## WHY USE PORN

The primary use for porn across all generations is not surprising—sexual arousal.

---

women-addicted-to-porn-stats/.

18. Pew Research Center, "Online Video 2013," https://www.pewresearch.org/internet/files/old-media/Files/Reports/2013/PIP_OnlineVideo2013.pdf.

19. Pew Research Center, "Online Video 2013," https://www.pewresearch.org/internet/files/old-media/Files/Reports/2013/PIP_OnlineVideo2013.pdf.

20. Proven Men Ministries, "Survey 2014: How many Christians do you think watch porn?," para. 1, https://www.prnewswire.com/news-releases/2014-survey-how-many-christians-do-you-think-watch-porn-271236741.html.

21 D. K. Braun-Courville and M. Rojas, "Exposure to sexually explicit Web sites and adolescent sexual attitudes and behaviors," in *The Journal Of Adolescent Health* 45.2 (2009) 156–62.

22. J. S. Carroll, L. M. Padilla-Walker, L. J. Nelson, C. D. Olson, C. M. Barry, and S. D. Madsen, "Generation XXX," in *Journal of Adolescent Research* 23.1 (2008) 6–30.

## Appendix 3

Other reasons found across generations include:

- to express my sexuality
- less risky than having sex
- set the mood with my significant other
- to get tips or ideas
- it's just fun
- curiosity
- boredom

What's insightful is looking at the four reasons to use porn after sexual arousal. They are exactly the same and in the exact same order for teens:

- to get tips or ideas
- it's just fun
- curiosity
- boredom

And among teens, "boredom" and "curiosity" are cited nearly twice as often as reasons than "it's just fun."[23] Boredom and curiosity seem the easiest reasons to overcome, but the numbers seem to reveal a lack of effort in fighting the use of porn.

The ongoing sexualization of our culture is reflected in generational differences in attitudes about porn.

> 73 percent of senior adults (fifty-five plus) consider porn morally unacceptable[24]
> 53 percent of adults (thirty-five to fifty-four) consider porn morally unacceptable[25]

On the other hand . . .

---

23. Barna, "The Porn Phenomenon [Summary]," number 2, https://www.barna.com/the-porn-phenomenon/.

24. Andrew Dugan, "More Americans Say Pornography Is Morally Acceptable," table 3, https://news.gallup.com/poll/235280/americans-say-pornography-morally-acceptable.aspx.

25. Andrew Dugan, "More Americans Say Pornography Is Morally Acceptable," graphic 1, https://news.gallup.com/poll/235280/americans-say-pornography-morally-acceptable.aspx.

# Appendix 3

5 percent of young adults (eighteen to twenty-four) say their friends consider viewing porn as bad[26]
11 percent of teens (thirteen to seventeen) say their friends consider viewing porn as bad[27]

Further insight is found when looking at "Things Considered Always or Usually Wrong by Teens and Young Adults" based on the five-point scale: always wrong, usually wrong, neither wrong or ok, usually ok, always ok.

> Things considered "Always" or "Usually Wrong":
> 88 percent—Taking something that belongs to someone else
> 75 percent—Having a romantic relationship with someone other than a spouse
> 71 percent—Saying something that isn't true
> 56 percent—Not recycling
> 55 percent—Thinking negatively about someone with a different point of view
> 48 percent—Overeating
> 38 percent—Significant consumption of electricity or water
> 32 percent—Wanting something that belongs to someone else
> 32 percent—Viewing pornographic images
> 27 percent—Reading erotic or pornographic content (no pictures)
> 24 percent—Watching sexually explicit scenes in TV or movies[28]

As attitudes change, so do actions. Sixty-two percent of teens and young adults report having received nude images via text, email, social media, or an app.[29] Fifty-one percent of teen and young adult users of porn have sent nude images the same way.[30] Thus, in fact, they become producers and distributors of porn themselves.

Bottom line, porn use in America is considered acceptable by most people, and becoming more so. It is being used by most Americans. At the same time, porn is growing in its portrayal of men as violent and dominant and women as submissive and enjoying the abuse they're receiving. In a study of the top fifty rented porn films, physical aggression occurred in 88 percent of scenes, while verbal aggression was portrayed in 48 percent

---

26. McDowell/Barna, "The Porn Phenomenon," 25.
27. McDowell/Barna, "The Porn Phenomenon," 25.
28. McDowell/Barna, "The Porn Phenomenon," 64.
29. McDowell/Barna, "The Porn Phenomenon," 28.
30. McDowell/Barna, "The Porn Phenomenon," 28.

of scenes.[31] Gonzo porn, an amateur porn style, is even worse. It portrays women as always ready for sex and enthusiastic to do whatever men want, irrespective of how painful, humiliating, or harmful it is.[32]

The internet connection to porn means that the more one uses porn, the more often they will be targeted through network ads that use cookies.

It's clear porn is prolific, growing, and becoming ever more violent. Now let's take a closer look at the harm that results from its use.

## How porn hurts everyone as well as women and children around the world:

The following are just a few examples of the harm caused by porn. Additional information can be found in the resources cited.

*Porn hurts the women and children used to produce it:*

They suffer verbal, physical and sexual abuse that inflicts long-term damage and, in some cases, lifelong damage.

*From the National Center for Biotechnology Information/National Library of Medicine—Aggression and Sexual Behavior in Best-Selling Pornography Videos: A Content Analysis:*

This current study analyzes the content of popular pornographic videos, with the objectives of updating depictions of aggression, degradation, and sexual practices and comparing the study's results to previous content analysis studies.

Findings reveal high levels of aggression in pornography in both verbal and physical forms.

Of the 304 scenes analyzed,

- 88.2 percent of scenes contained physical aggression, principally spanking, gagging, and slapping

---

31. Fight the New Drug, "Study Shows 88% Of Popular Porn Videos Contain Violence," para. 2, https://fightthenewdrug.org/popular-videos-violence/.

32 Dines, *Pornland*.

- 48.7 percent of scenes contained verbal aggression, primarily name-calling
- Perpetrators of aggression were usually male, whereas targets of aggression were overwhelmingly female. Targets most often showed pleasure or responded neutrally to the aggression.[33]

*Remember, this is where our young men are learning about sex and how to treat women and girls and where they are learning what are acceptable behaviors towards them.*

From TraffickingHub:
It's not just about what is portrayed on the screen. Behind the scenes, many young women sign up to be "amateur models" for easy money, without a real understanding of what they're really signing up for.[34] Or else they're invited and flown to modeling opportunities, only to learn way too late that it's actually a porn shoot.[35] In some cases, they are pushed into a world where female porn performers are given large amounts of drugs and alcohol to be more submissive in the videos and feel less pain.[36] This can pave the way to them developing addictions to these substances that keep them in the industry because of dependence.[37]

## Porn normalizes harmful behaviors

Porn normalizes and promotes illegal, harmful activity.

---

33. Ana J. Bridges et al., "Aggression and sexual behavior in best-selling pornography videos," Abstract, in *Violence Against Women* 16.10 (October 2010) 1065–85, https://pubmed.ncbi.nlm.nih.gov/20980228/.

34. Fight the New Drug, "Hot Girls Wanted: Netflix's Raw Amateur Porn Documentary," https://fightthenewdrug.org/hot-girls-wanted-netflixs-raw-amateur-porn-documentary/.

35. Fight the New Drug, "Hundred of Women Who Agreed to Model Swimsuits Were Forced to Perform in Porn, Lawsuit Alleges," https://fightthenewdrug.org/sex-on-camera-san-diego-porn-scheme/.

36. Fight the New Drug, "'You're Gonna Be A Star': The Day I was Drugged and Raped on a Porn Set," https://fightthenewdrug.org/youre-gonna-be-a-star-my-career-as-an-abused-porn-performer/.

37. Fight the New Drug, "10 Ex-Porn Performers Reveal the Brutal Truth Behind Their Most Popular Scenes," https://fightthenewdrug.org/10-porn-stars-speak-openly-about-their-most-popular-scenes/.

From TraffickingHub:
Rape, incest, and underage sexual activity are all exploited by the porn industry. In fact, the terms "stepmom," "stepsister," and "teen" are some of the most popular and frequently searched terms in pornography today. Nothing is off-limits in porn, even if it's harmful to our female family members, neighbors, and peers.[38]

In fact, *The Daily Beast* reported a 178 percent increase in the production of incest porn in recent years, making up one in ten porn purchases by young adults. This means preferences are shifting so even family members are being objectified through a twisted lens.[39]

Also, the portrayal of sexualized teenage schoolgirls in pornography is one of the most popular categories. While the actress might legally be above the age of consent, they are using illegal childhood sexual abuse as a way to entertain others and make money. Normalizing this behavior by showing it as a form of entertainment twists people's perspectives and preferences and can frequently lead to sexual abuse of minors.[40]

Dr. Mary Anne Layden, the director of the sexual trauma and psychopathology program at the University of Pennsylvania, said: "I've been a psychotherapist for 25 years. I specialize in the treatment of sexual violence victims and perpetrators and sex addicts. I spend all day, every day talking to rapists, and rape victims, pedophiles and incest survivors, sex addicts, pornography addicts, prostitutes, strippers, and pornography models. After I had done this work for about 10 years, I had a sudden realization that I hadn't treated one case of sexual violence that didn't involve pornography. You don't have to have a Ph.D. in psychology to realize something is going on here."[41]

## Porn harms its users, families, and society

Porn is addicting. A study by Cambridge University found the brain's response to sexually explicit cues were similar to the response in drug studies.

---

38. Fight the New Drug, "'Fauxcest': Why is Incest-Themed Porn Getting So Popular?," para. 1, https://fightthenewdrug.org/understanding-the-rise-of-incest-themed-porn/.

39. Fight the New Drug, "'Fauxcest': Why is Incest-Themed Porn Getting So Popular?," para. 3, https://fightthenewdrug.org/understanding-the-rise-of-incest-themed-porn/.

40. Fight the New Drug, "Understanding How Child Sexual Abuse Material is Used to Groom Abuse Victims," https://fightthenewdrug.org/porn-used-groom-abuse-victims/.

41. M. A. Layden, "Pornography and violence," in *The Social Costs of Pornography*, ed. J. R. Stoner and D. M. Hughes. Princeton: Witherspoon Institute, 2010.

# Appendix 3

Porn addicts in the study fit the addiction model, wanting more but not liking it more.[42] There are a number of studies showing how porn is addictive and what the results are. People who have a pornography addiction can spend as much as thirty-five to forty-five hours per week on the internet.[43]

Men were shown the same explicit film repeatedly. After time, they found it less arousing (they habituated to it) but, once exposed to a new film (novelty), their arousal increased to the same level as it was when first seeing the initial film. In short, the same old images become boring after awhile, so the body seeks new ones to keep its arousal up.[44] This builds the demand for the most abusive porn.

Jesse Logan, an eighteen-year-old high school senior from Ohio, sent a nude photo of herself to her boyfriend, who then made the decision to forward it to four other girls. The photo went viral, and Jesse was ostracized by her peers and quickly spun into an emotional depression. Taunted and labeled a "slut," a "whore," and a "porn queen," Jesse Logan hanged herself at her home a few months later.[45]

Obviously pornography should not be made with children or accessed by them, but the impact on them is changing the world as we know it.

According to the National Coalition for the Protection of Children & Families, in 2010, 47 percent of families in the United States reported that pornography is a problem in their home.[46] There's been exponential growth in porn since then, indicating the problem has gotten worse, not better.

Eleven is the average age a child is first exposed to porn; 94 percent of kids will see porn by age fourteen.[47]

Children whose brains are not fully developed are viewing porn and learning what sex should look like, how women should be treated, and

---

42. D. J. Mechelmans et. al., "Enhanced Attentional Bias Towards Sexually Explicit Cues in Individuals with and Without Compulsive Sexual Behaviors," *PLoS One*, August 25, 2014, 133–34. http://www.ncbi.nlm.nih.gov/pubmed/25153083.

43. A. Cooper, D. Delmonico, and R. Burg, "Cybersex users, abusers, and compulsives: New findings and implications," *Sexual Addiction & Compulsivity* 7.1 (2000) 5–29.

44. P. Banca et al., "Novelty, conditioning and attentional bias to sexual rewards," *Journal of Psychiatric Research* 72 (January 2016) 91–101.

45. Karen Peterson-Iyer, "Mobile Porn?: Teenage Sexting and Justice for Women," *Journal of the Society of Christian Ethics* 33.2 (Fall/Winter 2013) 93–110.

46. Family Research Council, "Pornography, America's Public Health Crisis," para. 4, https://www.frc.org/blog/2018/08/pornography-americas-public-health-crisis.

47. Darcel Rockett, "Kids are seeing porn sooner than adults think," para. 3, https://www.njherald.com/story/lifestyle/2018/04/08/kids-are-seeing-porn-sooner/4143839007/.

becoming desensitized to sexual abuse and violence. No doubt one of the results is child-on-child sexual abuse.

Statistics reveal as many as 40 percent of children sexually abused are abused by other children.[48] In fact, the younger a child victim is, the more likely the offender is another child.

Children are the perpetrators in 43 percent of abuse of children under six. Of these child offenders, 14 percent are under the age of twelve.[49] Parents need to know it's not a matter of *if* your child will see porn, but a matter of *when*.

## Porn and Racism

Pornography is rife with racist material that celebrates the degradation of black women and girls. Commercial sex buyers are predominantly white while victims of sex trafficking are disproportionately women and girls of color. Predators prey upon the people society has marginalized, which means minority communities are a prime target. The list goes on.[50]

According to porn star and adult film director James Deen, racism is rampant in the industry, both on camera and behind the scenes. "Interracial" is a popular subgenre of porn, and these scenes often trade on the racist idea that white women are violating themselves by having sex with a black man.[51]

According to Gail Dines, "Blatant examples of racism that were once commonplace in mainstream media have become less acceptable. But this is not so for the porn industry, which gets away with a level of racism that is breathtaking in its contempt and loathing of people of color."[52]

---

48. D. Finkelhor, "Characteristics of crimes against juveniles." Durham, NH: Crimes against Children Research Center, 2012.

49. H. N. Snyder, "Sexual Assault of Young Children as Reported to Law Enforcement: Victim, Incident, and Offender Characteristics." Washington, DC: U.S. Department of Justice, Office of Justice Programs, Bureau of Justice Statistics, 2000. http://www.ojp.usdoj.gov/bjs/pub/pdf/saycrle.pdf.

50. See the National Center on Sexual Exploitation (NCOSE), https://endsexualexploitation.org.

51. Rachel Bell, "James Deen Is Pissed Off About Racism in the Porn Industry," Vice.com, September 3, 2015, https://www.vice.com/en/article/wnwawq/james-deen-is-pissed-off-about-racism-in-the-porn-industry.

52. Dines, *Pornland*: How Porn Has Hijacked Our Sexuality (Boston: Beacon, 2011); see also Julie Bindel, "The Truth About the Porn Industry," *The Guardian*, July 2, 2010. http://www.theguardian.com/lifeandstyle/2010/jul/02/gail-dines-pornography.

For example, there are overtly racist titles that feature black men and an entire porn genre called "interracial." Roles and scenarios often rely on offensive racial stereotypes, such as black men cast as drug dealers or criminals. White women often refuse to do scenes with black men or ask for extra money to do so.[53]

## Porn fuels the sex trafficking, rape, and abuse of women and children globally

On its most basic level, using porn is engaging in prostitution or sex trafficking. The women and children we're using for our pleasure were either paid (prostitution), or forced, tricked, and/or are minors (sex trafficking). Porn use provides the funds to develop more porn and the need for more victims to be used in its production.

The bottom line is every time we use porn, we take part in the sexual abuse and rape of women and children.

We may think that watching a little porn alone at home doesn't have an impact on sex trafficking. Dr. Mahri Irvine, adjunct professional lecturer at American University, said: "I really wish that people who watch porn knew more about that. Because I think they believe that they're engaging in this activity in a very passive way. And they're like, 'Oh, I'm doing it in the privacy of my own home and this is just a video that I'm watching.' And they're not associating it with the fact that pornography is very often the filmed rape of sex trafficking victims."[54]

Noel Bouché, executive director of pureHOPE, explained: "While pornographic content includes trafficked victims from around the world, porn consumers aren't told anything about the performers, including which ones may have been trafficked from an early age. Regular users of internet pornography are likely consuming pornography that includes adult and child victims of sex trafficking."[55]

---

53. Dines, *Pornland*.

54. Charisma, "How Pornography is Linked to Human Trafficking," para. 12, https://mycharisma.com/spiritled-living/man-life/how-pornography-is-linked-to-human-trafficking/#:~:text=Mahri%20Irvine%2C%20Adjunct%20Professional%20Lecturer,in%20a%20very%20passive%20way.

55. Luke Gibbons, "The Porn Industry is Modern-day Slavery: How Pornography and Sex Trafficking Are Linked," para. 12, https://www.missionfrontiers.org/issue/article/the-porn-industry-is-modern-day-slavery-how-pornography-and-sex-trafficking.

## Appendix 3

In Shared Hope International's report on the demand for sex trafficking, pornography is seen as the primary gateway to the purchase of humans for commercial sex.[56]

Catherine Mackinnon, a professor at Harvard Law School, says that "consuming pornography is an experience of bought sex" and thus it creates a hunger to continue to purchase and objectify and act out what is seen.[57]

Let's look a little deeper into some evidence of how using porn, and the growing demand for it, fuels sex trafficking and the abuse of women and children.

Melissa Farley, PhD, founder and director of Prostitution Research and Education and a world-renowned expert in the field, has found that, in a very literal way, pornography is advertising for trafficking, not just in general, but also in the sense that traffickers and pimps use pornographic images of victims as specific advertising for their "products."[58]

Dr. Farley's research into men who buy women and children for sex found that "all of the men we interviewed acknowledged using pornography. Nearly all the interviewees in this research used pornographic videos (99%)."[59] Seventy-nine percent of the men interviewed in her research on the men who bought sex in Cambodia shared their sex acts with women in prostitution had changed over time. Most of the changes, they told us, came from viewing pornography and, to a lesser extent, the changes were a result of what they learned from friends. One sex buyer said, "Whenever I went for sex, I'd like to try new styles I had seen in sex movies . . ." As porn becomes more and more abusive, it results in greater abuse of the victims of sex trafficking.[60]

---

56 Shared Hope International, "Sex Trafficking: 'A Supply Answer to a Demand Problem,'" https://sharedhope.org/2019/12/02/blind-eyes-opened/.

57. Catharine A. Mackinnon, "Pornography as Trafficking," in *Pornography: Driving the Demand in International Sex Trafficking* by David E. Guinn and Julie DiCaro (Los Angeles: Captive Daughters Media, 2007) 31–42, 32.

58. Melissa Farley, *Prostitution and Trafficking in Nevada: Making the Connections.* San Francisco: Prostitution Research & Education, 2007, 153.

59. Melissa Farley, *Thorn in the Heart: Cambodian Men who Buy Sex*, San Francisco: prostitutionresearch.com, 2012, 25.

60. Farley, *Thorn in the Heart*, 26.

## Appendix 3

Victims of trafficking are used in the production of porn,[61] and many are trafficked for that purpose.[62] As mentioned above, the porn websites distributing porn are no longer the producers of it. Ninety percent of free porn websites and nearly 100 percent of pay porn websites buy their material rather than create it themselves.[63]

One of the most troubling stories to take place in the porn industry has to do with the growth of models on PornHub. In 2019, 98,000 models joined PornHub's verified model program, bringing their total to more than 130,000![64]

One of these "models" was a fifteen-year-old girl who was shown in over fifty-eight videos. The official Twitter account for the site even admitted to her being a verified model. This young girl was being trafficked, and the site still has her name posted as one of their trending categories.[65]

In Miami, two men, one of them a former police officer, were convicted of trafficking by victimizing aspiring models. Under the false promise of opportunities to book work, victims were lured in for a phony audition where they were required to consume and promote beverages on camera. Their drinks were laced with benzodiazepines. Once the drugs took effect, the women were raped and filmed, and the footage was sold all over the internet and in porn stores across the US.[66]

In another case, twenty-two women sued and won a lawsuit against a porn website because they were deceived and coerced into making porn. Part of the case was a production of child rape, sexual abuse, and trafficking of a minor. The owner fled the United States and is currently wanted by

---

61. Linda Smith and Cindy Coloma, *Renting Lacy: A Story of America's Prostituted Children*, Vancouver, WA: Shared Hope International, 2009, 15–25.

62. Victor Malarek, *The Johns: Sex for Sale and the Men Who Buy It*. Toronto: Key Porter, 2009, 203.

63. Matthew Zook, "Report on the location of the Internet adult industry," in *C'Lick Me: A Netporn Studies Reader*, ed. Katrien Jacobs, Marije Janssen, and Matteo Pasquinelli. (Amsterdam: Institute of Network Cultures, 2007), 103–21. http://www.networkcultures.org/_uploads/24.pdf.

64. Curtis Silver, "PornHub 2019 Year in Review Report: More Porn, More Often," para. 6, https://www.forbes.com/sites/curtissilver/2019/12/11/pornhub-2019-year-in-review-report-more-porn-more-often/?sh=1a3105974671.

65. Traffickinghub, https://traffickinghub.com/.

66. Kyle Munzenrieder, "Emerson Callum and Lavont Flanders Convicted of Making Rape Porn," *Miami New Times*, December 9, 2011, https://www.miaminewtimes.com/news/emerson-callum-and-lavont-flanders-convicted-of-making-rape-porn-6559908.

federal agents. The abuse of these twenty-two women could be found on other sites as well.[67]

Laila Mickelwait, the founder of the TraffickingHub campaign which is working to have PornHub shutdown, and already has over a million supporters,[68] shared, "there could be hundreds, if not thousands, of videos of underage sex trafficking victims on PornHub . . . we already have the evidence, and it is just the tip of the iceberg."[69]

## PORN AND THE CHURCH—HOW BAD IS IT?

On its most basic level, using porn is adultery. Jesus taught if we look at a woman with lust in our heart, we've committed adultery. Lusting happens when we look at porn; we don't have to be Bible scholars to understand using porn is a sin.

So what percentage of self-identified Christians are committing adultery?

First, let's define "Christian." Since we will be using the recent research by George Barna, we'll use his definition. Under Barna's definition, practicing Christians are self-identified Christians who agree strongly that their faith is very important in their life and have attended a church worship service within the past month. (Self-identified Christians who do not meet these criteria are called nonpracticing Christians.)[70]

- The percentage of Americans who use porn—51 percent
- The percentage of self-identified Christians who use porn—45 percent
- The percentage of practicing Christians who use porn—28 percent[71]

Note: Other research finds *64 percent of Christian men* and *15 percent of Christian women* say they watch porn at least once a month.[72]

67. Traffickinghub, https://traffickinghub.com/.

68. Traffickinghub, https://traffickinghub.com/.

69. Robert Knight, "Petition to Shut Down Largest Porn Site Gains More THan One Million Signers," Timothy Plan, August 19, 2020, https://blog.timothyplan.com/2020/08/petition-to-shut-down-largest-porn-site-gains-more-than-one-million-signers/#:~:text="At%20this%20very%20moment%2C%20there,the%20tip%20of%20the%20iceberg.

70. McDowell/Barna, *The Porn Phenomenon*, 45.

71. McDowell/Barna, *The Porn Phenomenon*, 47.

72. CovenantEyes, "Pornography Statistics," https://www.covenanteyes.com/pornstats/.

# APPENDIX 3

## Porn use and pastors

- 57 percent of pastors are currently struggling with, or have struggled with, porn use[73]
- 64 percent of youth pastors are currently struggling with, or have struggled with, porn use[74]

| Feelings about Porn Use | % of Pastors | % of Youth Pastors |
|---|---|---|
| Great Shame | 87% | 94% |
| Fear | 55% | 44% |
| Escape from Pressures | 53% | 44% |

Seventy percent of self-identified Christians say a pastor should leave ministry if he uses porn.[75]

## A Pastor's Story

A dear friend and former pastor has graciously allowed me to share his story, as he has written it.

*The thing that breaks my heart is so many men are struggling. Using porn makes you feel horrible, and you feel you have to lie . . . in a way, like Lance Armstrong, especially for pastors and key Christian leaders. You kind of start protecting yourself at all costs. The lies are subtle at first, but they become automatic, a way you stay sane and stay away from the shame and guilt of being discovered.*

*And then I obviously know its connection to trafficking which just adds to the pain. I remember when we were under cover in Cambodia, the mama-san said, "Pick your girl," I vividly remember looking out and thinking I'm ok, uh, and automatically thinking I want the one who's most attractive. I caught myself and was like whoa, what the hell! And had to face my own sin even in that moment, but was able to catch it, snap out if it. I share this to show the trafficking piece is hard, especially when you're still fully trapped in porn. It adds to the guilt and shame that's already crushing in weight.*

73. McDowell/Barna, *The Porn Phenomenon*, 80.
74. McDowell/Barna, *The Porn Phenomenon*, 80.
75. McDowell/Barna, *The Porn Phenomenon*, 114.

# Appendix 3

*I remember always feeling like I wasn't really free. I would have a James 5:16 moment and feel healing, but it's really a symptom or masking of a deeper pain that additionally becomes a powerful habit, an addiction. It's the two-part freedom piece, yeah you need Jesus and confession, but you need to deal with the root issues (that sadly most Christians don't even realize they have, not fully anyway).*

*So I did have a few pastor guys I could talk to, but it was always just enough information I'd give them. Then I'd end up messing up again and thinking I could never tell them it happened again.*

*There was a deafening silence; you'd struggle trying to speak up, but you knew you weren't going to. Fear is big. Then the shame is high, subconscious even. I found talking to other pastors unhelpful. They were in denial about their own struggle and we were unable to be helpful to each other. We were all needing help. Porn is a real taboo, but spoken of as if it's not. Easier to pray and move on, hoping to never bring it up again.*

*It's so hidden and shameful and embarrassing, it's really hard to be fully open with it as a pastor.*

*I remember getting asked in a large group of pastors if I wanted to share . . . I was raw and men were in tears, broken, bound, struggling, and scared. It was powerful and sad.*

*In short, I only really shared about it from a past-tense place when it was almost always current in some ways. And I found that to be true with most pastors honest enough to open up about it.* (Note: He's free today.)

## Conclusion

Porn use is no different in the church than in the rest of the world; it's everywhere. The COVID-19 pandemic is nothing compared the porn pandemic in the church.

Fear, shame, and guilt keep porn use hidden in the church—it's Satan's perfect tool.

Of course it's bad news that porn is so prevalent in the church. But there's good news buried in it (Rom 8:28). We can become a movement that can result in the protection of women and children around the world . . . and without leaving home. And the reality is this: like most issues our society faces today, this is a heart issue more than a legal issue. Activism and awareness outside the church provides limited success because most of the time it doesn't deal with the issue of demand. Also, it is not based upon

# APPENDIX 3

the agreement of what is wrong as revealed in God's Word or the power of God's Word to transform hearts and to help us guard our hearts (Prov 4:23).

Every day our hearts (as the Bible reveals, the seat of our thoughts, emotions, and will) are under attack from our flesh, our culture, and Satan. Victory comes as, united in the power of Christ, we work together to defeat this.

I have great respect for the efforts of our partners in the fight against sex trafficking. Exodus Cry and their work with TraffickingHub has brought global awareness of PornHub's involvement in sex trafficking, with over one million signatures on their petition to shut PornHub down. I support their effort. It's a noble cause and effective to a point. However, if they reach total success in shutting down PornHub, but the demand is not reduced, someone else will meet it. Consider the shutting down of BackPage, an online source to buy sex. It did not reduce the sale of women and children because the demand was still there.

## HOW THE CHURCH OVERCOMES THE PORN PANDEMIC

In most cases, there's no need to start new programs or spend a bunch of money to have an impact at home and around the world. But, we do need to bring the fight against porn into our existing ministries.

Here's how we can get started:

*The Beginning of Awareness*

The entire church needs to know what you now know. The words of William Wilberforce ring true in the fight against porn: "You may choose to look the other way but you can never say again that you did not know."[76] Without a doubt, the most effective means, really the only effective means, is the senior or lead pastor during weekend services. This begins the process of awareness.

Of course he/she won't be able to share all the information in this appendix because of its length and sensitivity. However, he/she can begin

---

76. Pray for Harvard Law, "Quotes from William Wilberforce That Are Guaranteed to Inspire You," number 2, https://www.christianunion.org/ministries/universities/harvard-law/pray-for-harvard-law/995-pray-for-harvard-law-may2015.

the process from the pulpit and provide each adult attender resources to learn more. What's of utmost importance is changing the atmosphere surrounding porn. Users who are willing to admit their use and need for help to overcome it should not fear shame and guilt, but instead be considered heroes for their courage to stand and fight.

Awareness continues in all ministry programs as well as providing access to the resources needed in this fight. A few specific resources can be found in Appendix 3. But, generally speaking, our best tools are . . .

- the Holy Spirit
- God's Word
- Prayer
- Knowledge
- Love/Compassion
- Accountability

Actions:

Porn users generally fall into two categories: the uninformed and the addicted. I was an uninformed user and understanding its harm was enough to stop me from using porn. The more I learned, the more I became engaged in the fight against porn.

For the Uninformed:

- Education/Awareness:

    Age-appropriate information should be provided through all ministries. In some cases, this is best delivered by parents. Experts recommend starting conversations with youth about pornography around age nine.

- Accountability: This should begin with teens but could start even younger depending on smartphone use.

    » Restricted Access
    » Filtering and Accountability Software
    » Removal of Internet Access

## Appendix 3

- » Get Help (Counseling)
- » Accountability Partner
- Advocacy:

Provide the tools and encouragement needed to help individuals have the courage to speak up to others about the fight against porn and why it's so important.

## For the Addicted:

- Compassion
- Freedom Tools (See Appendix 3b for the steps one man took to find freedom and the tools he used.)
  - » Addiction is often categorized by the 4 C's:
    - Continued use is spite of negative consequences
    - Compulsion to use
    - Inability to Control use
    - Craving—psychological or physical
- Accountability
  - » Restricted Access
  - » Filtering and Accountability Software
  - » Removal of Internet Access
  - » Get Help (Counseling)
  - » Accountability Partner

# APPENDIX 3a

## Addiction

**THE BRAIN**[1]

Addiction is a diagnosis that no one wants to get. It destroys families, relationships, turns one away from God, and leads to death. Most addicts have some type of genetic likelihood or family history of addiction. A scary finding is that an individual who has no predisposition to addiction is still at risk when it comes to pornography. Addiction is the brain being altered to think, "I have got to have it no matter what it is." This "it" can be drugs, alcohol, fatty foods, porn, and a variety of other things.

**THE REWARD CIRCUIT**

Prefrontal cortex

Our brains are wired with something scientists call the reward circuit. This circuit affects mood, emotions, desires, drives, love/bonding, and addiction. When this part of the brain gets altered most, mental and physiological issues take place. Chemical and structural changes have larger impacts which will affect the individual in profound ways. The reward circuit could be seen as "seek pleasure and avoid pain."

Sex, eating, and bonding are all activities that involve the reward circuit. New ideas and experiences spark the reward circuit; as the brain learns from these new adventures, it wires the brain to seek more. This is why we

---

1. See "Your Brain on Porn: How Internet Porn Affects the Brain," (video, 2015) https://www.yourbrainonporn.com/videos/your-brain-on-porn-how-internet-porn-affects-the-brain-2015/.

## Appendix 3A

seek out hours of information on YouTube, news sites, biblical studies, and sexual experiences. When we see a new type of dessert, food, or ice cream the reward circuit will spark and think, "I have got to have it no matter what it is." When the reward circuit gets out of balance our appetite does as well, whether for substances or sexual.

The power of the reward circuit is found in the chemical dopamine that is released when the brain thinks, "I have got to have it no matter what it is." Fatty food, porn, drugs, novelty, news, games, information, etc. are all releasers of dopamine. Take away dopamine and you take away motivation. Dopamine relates to wanting, seeking, and craving, but not from the enjoyment of the act. Once the act happens the brain releases opioids, which creates a satisfaction to no longer seek the "it." Orgasm releases a large quantity of opioids, which puts a check on the dopamine so that we slow down our seeking of a craving. Dopamine is stronger than opioids, which means we seek more than we are satisfied. Dopamine levels in the brain are highest in sexual pleasure but can be altered by drugs such as morphine and cocaine. Some drugs release higher levels of dopamine than others. Drugs hijack the natural by adding the same substance in a chemical form and can majorly rewire the brain. Sexual novelty, which comes through porn, keeps dopamine surging. It produces a constant flow that keeps the user in a state of searching. Every mouse click is to a new video which produces the flow of dopamine causing the user's brain to rewire and seek "it" no matter what.

Humans were designed to store calories and produce offspring. This means that when the body has access to food it will eat a lot of it because there could be a shortage. When the body has access to the conditions to reproduce (create offspring) it will crave it until reproduction is achieved. Mice will not behave monogamously because their species needs many to survive. If a mouse has one partner he will no longer reproduce once the partner is known and is producing offspring. But introduce another female mouse and his libido will swing up until successful breeding has taken place; this will continue indefinitely. Rams, monkeys, and humans' sexual drives all spike when a new sexual partner is introduced. This is called the Coolidge effect. In the natural world and the biblical model man is designed for one woman and vice versa. Porn is stimulating the brain as a new sexual partner would. Our brains are wired to reproduce and create offspring and porn fakes the brain into thinking that a new partner is available; this releases dopamine over and over again.

## Appendix 3A

The brain is also wired to desire the supernormal stimulus that porn offers; this includes exaggerated features, fake orgasms, and unrealistic scenarios. This violation of expectation gets dopamine soaring which causes a great addictive feeling. Sexual conditioning begins to take place: the user is learning how to have sex, what sexual acts are stimulating, and creating fetishes, extreme desires, or losing interest in actual sex with a spouse. Other chemicals start getting released with shock and surprise, anxiety, and extreme situations. The user will begin to get brainwashed into new preferences and desire, lowering the view of women, introducing rape myths, and even creating a sexual desire for younger people.

Addiction-related brain changes will also, to some degree, affect the user. These changes could result in addiction, erectile dysfunction, or a rewired libido.[2,3]

After the brain is conditioned by porn it will no longer go back to a pre-porn state. Think of the conditioning like a hiking trail: it starts out with a trailblazer going for the first time, and after many hikes and years of use the pathway is clear and vegetation will leave the path alone. There is good news though. The pathway, when ignored, won't be on the mind all the time. Another chemical in this process is called DeltaFosB. This is a chemical that keeps your thoughts on something. Abstaining for eight weeks, DeltaFosB weakens the circuits that have been made by the porn trail. Quitting gets easier after this time goes by, and the user can find more success in staying porn-free. But just like an alcoholic, the path can be visited any time, and the power of addiction can be reignited.

Drugs and food have limits to consumption; humans will get sick or overdose if appetite is taken to the extreme. The difference with porn is that no physical restrictions are in place. The internet has become a dopamine machine—click and get it. Dopamine is used for novelty, which helps us survive, grow, and seek; but what happens when all that is novel is just coming from one source, internet porn?

---

2. Lucia O'Sullivan et al., "A Longitudinal Study of Problems in Sexual Functioning and Related Sexual Distress Among Middle to Late Adolescents," *Journal of Adolescent Health* 59.3 (September 2016) 318–24.

3. K. Sutton, "Patient Characteristics by Type of Hypersexuality Referral: A Quantitative Chart Review of 115 Consecutive Male Cases," *Journal of Sex and Marital Therapy* 41.6 (September 2, 2014) 563–80.

## Appendix 3A

Addiction is often categorized by the 4 C's:
Continued use is spite of negative consequences
Compulsion to use
Inability to Control use
Craving: psychological or physical

Drug, alcohol, and porn addiction all show the same brain use. The user still feels the need to look and seek but does not want to.

# APPENDIX 3b
## Caleb Miller, CEO and Co-Founder of Regenerate

*Caleb struggled with an addiction to pornography for fifteen years, with many failed attempts at quitting. He recognized that he would never find freedom if he didn't treat his addiction like the big problem that it was and seriously look for help. It was a difficult and self-revealing journey to recovery, but Caleb has now been free from pornography since 2015. Over the last two years, Caleb has acted as co-leader of sexual integrity support groups, and accountability friend and mentor to men seeking sexual integrity. He assisted in founding Regenerate (501c3) in 2018, with the mission of assisting men, women, and children who have been entrapped in the sex industry into a life of freedom and integrity through Christ's love and gospel. Currently Caleb's goal is to equip churches with the tools and training needed to prevent sex trafficking within their communities, by mobilizing congregations to invest personally in the lives of the vulnerable and providing support for men seeking sexual integrity. Visit Regeneratewebsite.org to learn more about this ministry.*

### STARTING RECOVERY

#### Friend/Mentor

If you desire freedom from sex addiction of any kind, including pornography, it is extremely important to do something about it right *now*. The motivation you feel right now is a door that won't stay open forever. You need to get help now, while you are motivated, so that when you are no longer motivated you are already on your road to recovery and have safeguards in place.

Where should you start? You need to talk to somebody. Whether a friend or mentor, you need to start with confessing your struggle and asking for accountability. This is the hardest part and yet, absolutely necessary if you desire freedom and healing. It is important to choose someone who believes that freedom from sex addiction is possible and someone you feel you can trust. You don't have to confess every dark secret you have about your addiction in the first meeting. You just want to make them aware of your struggle and to ask them if they are willing to keep you accountable. The goal is to start an ongoing relationship where you can safely talk about your struggles and find encouragement to keep fighting. As your friendship deepens and trust for each other grows, you will naturally share more and more. Sex addiction grows like weeds in shame and secrecy. Having a friend walk this journey with you will start to remove the shame and allow you to start to deal with what is really going on in your heart.

How should you start? Start off strong, while you are motivated to find help. Go way beyond what you think you need to do to be free from addiction. When I came clean to my wife about my addiction, I didn't stop there. I found two accountability partners, gave them a lengthy list of questions to ask me every week, looked for a counselor, went to a retreat for men struggling with sex addiction, and found a support group. What was my struggle? Pornography, which I had stopped looking at a year and a half before, but rather than allowing my mind to tell me it wasn't a big deal, I got help. I had been enslaved to pornography long enough; I didn't want to chance going back to it again.

It's really important to remember on your journey to recovery, that you are responsible for your recovery, not your accountability friend or mentor, not your counselor, or your support group, or an app on your phone. You. You can absolutely find freedom from your addiction and you are responsible for finding it.

## Support Groups

Although an accountability friend or mentor should be at the top of your priority list, finding a good sexual integrity support group to plug into can have a huge impact on your healing process and your journey to freedom. Support groups broaden your accountability network, allow people who are further along on their road to recovery to speak into your life, allow you to form healthy, deep, open, and honest relationships with other men who are also desiring freedom, connect you to helpful resources and materials

## Appendix 3B

that challenge your perspective and worldviews, and connect you to trusted counselors. Finding a support group can sometimes be difficult because they are confidential. You could start by looking into whether or not your church or other churches in your area have existing sexual integrity support groups. Another option is to look up counselors, chaplains, coaches, ministries, or activists in your area focused on sex addiction, reach out to them, and ask them if they have a list of recommended support groups in your area.

Beware of support groups that require you to share more than you are comfortable with, shame you, or seem to twist your arm into recovery. There should also be an agreement of confidentiality among all members. The best support groups are just a few individuals who act as accountability friends/mentors for each other. Again remember that it is not up to the support group to ensure you are fighting for freedom. You are the one who is fighting from addiction because you want to be free. Support groups are designed to encourage one another to break addiction and walk together on the way to recovery.

If you find that no support groups exist or fit with a proper method of healing, starting one is a good idea that will greatly benefit you and others. Expertise in sexual addiction is not needed to start a group, only willing people who want to fight for recovery together. Caleb recommends using, "a big curriculum that is very instructional and will take a long time to go through. This will give your group time to build consistency, provides a good model, and reduces the need for one person to actually be in charge." After the group has begun to take shape the material can be changed to best fit the needs of the groups. Be sure to try and establish a way to check in with each other outside of the group to encourage one another. "Sex addiction curriculum can be very heavy in psychology regarding addiction, which is helpful, but other books can keep things fresh and meet areas of need that otherwise would be missed. For example, utilizing books/resources regarding conflict resolution, relationships, fear/anxiety, and the heart of man can be super helpful to address specific areas that the group as a whole seem to struggle with."

Online and Local Support Groups

1. Harvest USA—https://harvestusa.org/
   My training as a leader in a sex addiction support group here in Pennsylvania was based in their leadership training materials. Good resource for curriculum.

2. Pure Desire Ministries—https://puredesire.org/
   Heard great things about them and it looks like a really good resource, but I have not personally used it.

Curriculum for Small Group

3. A L.I.F.E. Recovery Guide For Men—Mark Laaser, PhD
   A great starter for a support group. Literally all that is needed is people, a few who can read and follow instructions, and the book. It will take at least a year to go through, maybe longer.
4. Extinguishing The Flames, Fighting The Fire of Human Trafficking—MATTOO
   A workbook for support groups, focusing on the connection between addiction and trafficking.
5. Heart of Man—Movie and participants guide
   Excellent and thought-provoking. Short artistic representation of the prodigal son/sexual sin, small participants guide that takes a few weeks to go through with a group. Good for digging into the deep desires of the heart and recognizing emotional triggers. https://heartofmanmovie.com/store/.

## Counseling/Coaching

Your struggle to be sexually pure goes much deeper than just bad behavior that you need to kick. Your actions are only the tip of the iceberg. Your addiction is intimately tied to deep heart desires, deeply rooted beliefs about yourself, others, and God, and emotional triggers that likely started with your heart desires being unmet or trampled at some point in your past. Just trying to brush away the bad behavior will not deal with the much larger issue in your heart, and will, in many cases, not be successful.

Growing in your awareness and understanding of your emotional triggers, your deeply rooted beliefs, and your heart desires which are connected with your sex addiction and possibly other addictions you struggle with too, is a very important step. One way to do this is to ask yourself what you were feeling before you were tempted and why, then record your answers. After about one or two weeks you will probably start to see a clear pattern connecting specific emotions or mindsets with increased temptation. Once you recognize this pattern you can start to reach out for accountability before it leads to temptation and work on responding to these emotions/mindsets differently. Counseling or coaching can be extremely helpful in growing this awareness as well.

There is no perfect counselor. Each will have his strengths and his weaknesses, so just pick someone you feel comfortable with and seems to be the best fit for your current struggle. I recommend you start your search looking for sex addiction counselors or trauma counselors, rather than general counselors. You will probably find them more helpful. Please note again, it is not the counselor's job to fight for your freedom, that is again on you. They can help grow your understanding of your struggle and give you tools, but you are the one who has to fight.

Counselors/Experts

1. Gene McConnell—http://www.authenticrelationshipsint.com/about-gene/. Great guy! Lots of experience. Great approach.
2. Dan Allender—https://theallendercenter.org/find-a-counselor/. Great resource to counselors and survivors of childhood trauma.
3. Kenneth Taylor—http://www.mmacounseling.com/kennethtaylor.html. Worked in Phnom Penh, has a lot of experience, and started original sex addiction group for missionaries in Phnom Penh.

## Proactive Accountability

There are two levels of accountability. When you first start on your road toward recovery, accountability will probably look more like confession to your friend on a regular basis. This is level one accountability and it is good and necessary in the beginning of your journey. Level one accountability, however, is not where you want to stay. As you grow more aware of your emotional triggers through counseling, coaching, or other means, you will want to start reporting to your accountability partner when and why you are being triggered, rather than just reporting when you fall to temptation. This is what I call "proactive accountability." Proactive accountability will give you a chance to start working together with your accountability friend on finding helpful ways of dealing with your triggers and give your friend a heads-up that he needs to check in with you more than usual and to be praying for you. For example: when I have a fight with my wife and feel extremely misunderstood, I know now that I tend to be tempted more when

I feel misunderstood, so I reach out to my accountability friend right away to let him know that I will probably have more temptation over the next three days. He talks with me over the phone about my fight with my wife and helps provide perspective on the situation and encourages me to go for a walk to help me clear my head and calm down. I do and then am able to reconcile with my wife. My accountability partner still checks in on me over the next three days like I asked him to, but I'm much less likely to fall to temptation at this point. This is the type of accountability you should strive for.

## PRACTICAL STEPS

We were designed by God for relationships and sex addiction is trying to cope with the difficulties that can be part of them. Sexual addiction is in essence a relationship disorder; by making positive steps in strengthening relationships with those around you healthy results will follow. Invest in your wife, children, family, church, friends, or seek healthy new relationships and you will begin to see an improvement in your fight against temptation.

As stated above, your brain has been affected by sexual addiction or habits, thus your brain is going to desire other ways for dopamine to be released. Prayer, exercise, eating healthy, learning a new hobby, and music are other methods that are known to produce similar experiences that will help the brain. These activities are not sexual but will help fill the void that the unhealthy sexual practices have taken in the past.

Miller testifies to the power that God's word takes in breaking sin and following Jesus.

> Romans 12:2, Do not conform to the pattern of this world, but be transformed by the renewing of your mind. Then you will be able to test and approve what God's will is—his good, pleasing and perfect will.

This passage is so true and totally applicable to finding freedom from sin, but the goal in this passage and for us is not just to be free from sin, but to test and approve what God's will is, his good, pleasing, and perfect will.

One super practical way to renew your mind is reading the Bible, believing it even if it doesn't seem to fit with what you see in your life, and applying what you see taught, even if you don't understand it. By doing this you remove yourself from being in charge of your life and you demonstrate your faith in Jesus, your King, and that what he says is true and good. This cultivates a heart that wants to be transformed by Jesus. (Matthew 7:24)

## TOOLS AND RESOURCES

A tool is essential in getting a job done; but a hammer is not a house. Healing takes time, and tools are helpful in completing the project, but they should never be seen as the solution. They will help you move forward, but please be cautious, as they will seldom get to the heart of the matter. If you begin to depend on them for your freedom you will find ways around them. They should be used as road signs and speed bumps, allowing you to take measure of what is going on to address the problem that is triggering you to run to sexual addiction. If a dependency is placed on these tools when a new problem or addiction is at hand there will be nothing to stop you. Use the tools, but use them in community and part of the healing process.

Due to both religious and secular people wanting to quit porn there has been an out flowing of apps and blockers on the market. Some offer counseling, create groups, and have meditational programs. Please use caution, as they will take a secular approach and focus on self-improvement. Change is possible, but without a heart change that only God can bring you will only find a temporary solution. Jesus is the answer and we must rely on him to break the chains of sin that no one else can; he is the true savior.

For an in-depth study and a Christian perspective we recommend Covenant Eyes. It has resources that are great for pastors and laypeople and offers them for free. They also have a paid program that can be installed on computers and smartphones that helps assist with accountability. Every time you go to a site that leads to sexual temptation they send an email to your accountability partner. This helps slow down temptation and work out shortcomings with your friend or mentor who is helping you fight for freedom. Another similar service is offered by Accountable2you, which does the same thing.

A free service for computers is called K9. It sets up a program that many schools and organizations use to block adult content. See Appendix 3a.

## HOW TO TALK TO KIDS

The last resource we would like to give you is how to talk to your kids about sex and address the issue of pornography. No matter the age of your children it is not too late to talk to your kids about pornography. The average age kids first see porn is eleven years old. Covenant Eyes has some resources and is based in a Christian worldview. Culture Reframed is a secular organization but offers free online courses that help you talk about pornography with tweens and teens. We would recommend starting with the Covenant Eyes resources but if you need more please check out Culture Reframed (just please note that not all their views will represent a Christian worldview).

# APPENDIX 3c

## Recommended Resources: What/Where They Are/How to Get Them

**TEN OTHER GREAT RESOURCES**

1. Covenant Eyes—An organization that is dedicated to defeating pornography. They have an app for accountability, resources for porn's effects, how to quit porn, family protection, support for couples, and resources for pastors. These resources come in the form of free ebooks that are highly valuable to Christians. There are ten free ebooks here that are helpful and Christ-centered. They cover every area where we are focused and offer resources and a network for help.
2. *Wired for Intimacy: How Pornography Hijacks the Male Brain*—William M. Struthers
   a. "... common spiritual approaches of more prayer and accountability groups are often of limited help. In this book neuroscientist and researcher William Struthers explains how pornography affects the male brain and what we can do about it. Because we are embodied beings, viewing pornography changes how the brain works, how we form memories and make attachments. By better understanding the biological realities of our sexual development, we can cultivate healthier sexual perspectives and interpersonal relationships . . ."[1]

---

1. *Wired for Intimacy* Amazon description, https://www.amazon.com/Wired-Intimacy

## Appendix 3C

3. *How Pornography Harms: What Today's Teens, Young Adults, Parents, and Pastors Need to Know*—John D. Foubert, PhD. An indictment of the pornography industry and a complete resource demonstrating why people should avoid porn and how parents can guide their children. Website has author speak about each chapter and updates statistics as they come out.
4. *Your Brain on Porn: Internet Pornography and the Emerging Science of Addiction*—Gary Wilson
   a. https://www.yourbrainonporn.com/videos-articles/
5. Exodus Cry—"Exodus Cry is committed to abolishing sex trafficking and breaking the cycle of commercial sexual exploitation while assisting and empowering its victims."[2]
   a. Films
   b. Journal/Blog/Resources
   c. TraffickingHub.com
6. *Samson and the Pirate Monks* by Nate Larkin—A book about a pastor who was addicted to pornography . . . it is a story of redemption, people in the church came alongside him.
7. *Pure Desire* by Ted Roberts—and accompanying Seven Pillars Workbook. "Learn how to establish healthy personal boundaries with proven, practical applications to claim Christ's healing power and presence."[3]
8. *Every Man's Battle* by Stephen Arterburn and Fred Stoeker—"Millions have found *Every Man's Battle* the single greatest resource for overcoming the struggle and remaining strong in the face of temptation. With extensive updates for a new generation, this phenomenal bestseller shares the stories of dozens who have escaped the trap of sexual immorality and presents a practical, detailed plan for any man who desires sexual integrity. Includes a comprehensive workbook and a special section for women, designed to help them understand and support the men they love."[4]

---

-Pornography-Hijacks-Brain/dp/0830837000#:~:text=Countless%20Christian%20men%20struggle%20with,we%20can%20do%20about%20it.

2. Exodus Cry, "Our Solution," https://exoduscry.com/oursolution/.

3. *Pure Desire* OverDrive description, https://www.overdrive.com/media/1814824/pure-desire.

4. *Every Man's Battle* Amazon description, https://www.amazon.com/Every-Mans-Battle-Winning-Temptation/dp/0307457974.

9. *Finally Free* by Heath Lambert—In *Finally Free*, Dr. Heath Lambert, a leader in the biblical counseling movement, lays out eight gospel-centered strategies for overcoming the deceitful lure of pornography. Each chapter clearly demonstrates how the gospel applies to this particular battle and how Jesus can move readers from a life of struggle to a life of purity.
10. *Treating Pornography Addiction: The Essential Tools For Recovery* by Dr. Kevin Skinner—This book carefully walks someone struggling with pornography through the steps to recovery.

## TALKING TO YOUR KIDS ABOUT PORNOGRAPHY

1. Covenant Eyes—"Confident: Helping Parents Navigate Online Exposure" is a step-by-step conversation guide.

2. Culture Reframed—"Culture Reframed responds to the pornography crisis by providing education and support to promote healthy child and youth development. Our research-driven parent programs teach parents and those in the helping professions how to recognize and respond to the role pornography can play in sexual violence, unhealthy relationships, habitual use of porn, negative self-image, sexual dysfunction, depression, sexually transmitted infections, injuries, and other issues."[5]

3. Fight the New Drug Article: What To Do If Your Child Is Exposed To Porn

## ACCOUNTABILITY SOFTWARE

Used with a friend or mentor in order to keep track of website and video history in order to bring accountability and freedom from adult content.

1. Covenant Eyes
2. Accountable2you
3. XXXChurch

---

5. Culture Reframed, "About," https://culturereframed.org/about/.

APPENDIX 3C

## Apps and software

Fortify—The Fortify program was developed by a group that has a very popular anti-porn website, Fight the New Drug. This site and app are secular but rely on science to break addiction.

Brain Buddy iOS—"Brainbuddy rewires your brain, helping you create healthy new synaptic pathways that free you from porn addiction. Forever."[6] Self-help secular program to break addiction.

## Counseling App

"rTribe" smartphone app—Online counseling, coaching, and healing in community. Does offer Christian services.

## Blockers for PC

1. Free—K9 Web Protection—K9 Web Protection is the perfect solution for anybody who is conscious about online security. If you are a parent, you can use it to protect your children from accessing the more harmful online content. If you run a company, then you can use it to help counter corporate security threats. You can also use it to block spyware and malware on your machine, and also to keep you updated about online scams. K9 Web Protection works in real time to keep itself updated about new kinds of suspicious content online.

### GREAT ORGANIZATIONS

1. The Pink Cross—a ministry rescuing people from the porn industry.

2. National Center on Sexual Exploitation—a mission to defend human dignity and to oppose sexual exploitation.

3. Fight the New Drug—"Fight the New Drug is a non-religious and non-legislative organization that exists to provide individuals the opportunity to make an informed decision regarding pornography by

---

6. Ships Psychology, "Sexual Health Resources," https://www.shipspsychology.com.au/resources-sexual-health.

raising awareness on its harmful effects using only science, facts, and personal accounts."[7]

4. Setting Captives Free—Setting Captives Free exists to help men and women to freedom through the gospel of Jesus Christ.

5. Celebrate Recovery—"Celebrate Recovery is a Christ-centered, 12 step recovery program for anyone struggling with hurt, pain or addiction of any kind. Celebrate Recovery is a safe place to find community and freedom from the issues that are controlling our lives."[8]

## RESOURCES THAT INFLUENCED THE VIEWS AND EVIDENCED IN THIS REPORT

1. *The Journal of Treatment and Prevention*
   a. "The Development and Deployment of the Idea of Porn Addiction Within American Evangelicalism"[9]
   b. "Religion, Spirituality, and Sexual Addiction: A Critical Evaluation"[10]
   c. "Surfing for Sexual Sin: Relations Between Religiousness and Viewing Sexual Content Online"
2. Melissa Farley
   a. "'Renting an Organ for Ten Minutes:' What Tricks Tell Us about Prostitution, Pornography, and Trafficking"
   b. "Comparing Sex Buyers With Men Who Do Not Buy Sex: New Data on Prostitution and Trafficking"
3. Donna M. Hughes
   a. "Welcome to the Rape Camp: Sexual Exploitation and the Internet in Cambodia"
4. Catherine A. MacKinnon
   a. "Pornography as Trafficking"[11]

7. Fight the New Drug, "Who is Fight the New Drug?," https://fightthenewdrug.org/who-is-fight-the-new-drug/.

8. Christ's Chapel, "Celebrate Recovery: Freedom from Hurts, Habits and Hangups," http://www.christschapel.net/celebraterecovery#:~:text=Celebrate%20Recovery%20is%20a%20Christ,a%20bible%20based%20Recovery%20group.

9. Growing belief among evangelicals seems to observe higher rates of perceived porn addiction.

10. Religion has been shown to have positive effects when tempering sexual deviance.

11. A strong argument that porn and prostitution is the same thing, Pornography then

## Appendix 3C

5. Raymond CATW
    a. "The Consequences of the Sex Industry in the EU," Public hearing at the European Parliament, January 19, 2014.[12]
6. Research by Drew A. Kingston, Paul Fedoroff, Philip Firestone, Susan Curry, and John M. Bradford
    a. "Pornography use and sexual aggression: the impact of frequency and type of pornography use on recidivism among sexual offenders"[13]
7. A. J. Luzwick
    a. "Human Trafficking and Pornography: Using the Trafficking Victims Protection Act to Prosecute Trafficking for the Production of Internet Pornography"[14]
8. Yaman Akdeniz
    a. *Internet Child Pornography and the Law: National and International Responses*[15]
9. Monique Mattei Ferraro, Eoghan Casey, and Michael McGrath
    a. Investigating Child Exploitation and Pornography: The Internet, the Law and Forensic Science[16]

---

further creates demand for prostitution, hence for trafficking, through its consumption. Consuming pornography is an experience of bought sex, of sexually using a woman or a girl or a boy as an object who has been purchased. As such, it stimulates demand for buying women and girls and boys as sexual objects in the flesh in the same way it stimulates the viewer to act out on other live women and girls and boys the specific acts that are sexualized and consumed in the pornography.

12. The sex industry thrives on renamings its sexual exploitation as sex. Pornography is called erotica or adult videos; prostitution is renamed as sex work or sexual services; pimps are now called third-party business managers or erotic entrepreneurs; and lap dancing or sex clubs are called gentlemen's entertainment. Stats are good, but over fourteen years old. Legalization has proved unsuccessful and created more problems for women and higher trafficking numbers, not less.

13. Heavy read on the likelihood that violent offenders will reoffend after watching porn.

14. Legal justification to prosecute forced porn under the TVPA.

15. Looks at the legal fight against child pornography around the world, the growing need to fight across nations, and the role ISPs (internet service providers) play; does not put down porn across the board but its arguments against child porn seem just as valid for adult porn. Explains the process by which children are exposed to CP (child porn) and how that can create manipulative situations where the child will be more vulnerable to sexual advances. Gives a brief history of grooming.

16. Legal book containing case studies, etc.

10. Gene McConnell—http://www.authenticrelationshipsint.com/about-gene/
11. Dan Allender—https://theallendercenter.org/find-a-counselor/
12. Kenneth Taylor—http://www.mmacounseling.com/kennethtaylor.html.

www.ingramcontent.com/pod-product-compliance
Lightning Source LLC
Chambersburg PA
CBHW032150160426
43197CB00008B/845